Take The Lead

by

Miller Caldwell

ISBN – 978-1-910256-21-3

Contents

DEDICATION

In the pages of this book many dogs and their lives are recorded. However there are three special dogs worthy of a separate dedication. They have impacted on my life to a greater extent, opened my eyes and sharpened my appreciation of their canine world. It is to each of them I dedicate this book.

Firstly, I thank you Glen (1947-1964) the loyal guardian Border collie and friend who introduced me to the canine world from birth. To the same breed in Tâche (1991-2005) whose wisdom exceeded all others; whose loyalty to the family was unquestionable and his willingness to learn was so very special. Finally to Bobby (2003 -2014) a black Labrador who was not mine. I walked him most days for eight years and the bond of friendship, trust and workmanship became unequalled. All three dogs have been very special dogs indeed. Long will they be remembered by those they knew.

ACKNOWLEDGEMENTS

There are many to thank for this story of my life with dogs, because many of the dogs were not mine but theirs.

Scott, Jane, Shannon and Ronan Dunbar for Bobby; Frank and Christina Dunbar for Buck. Dr Meg Manson and Jim Manson for providing Tâche; Joan and Watson Linton for Ben. Bruce and Elly Caldwell for Hilda; the un-named nurse and doctor now in New Zealand who had to donate Czar to us: Alan and Margaret Nicolson for Ziggy; and Alistair and Shona Harkness for Blu.

My father's notes about Glen before I was born have been invaluable, especially as he was not a natural dog lover. Yet he was proud to be called to that profession which daily wore a dog-collar. His notes in Part I of this book make Glen talk. Thereafter the book resorts to the third person.

Finally my appreciation goes to Diak and the nameless rabid dog. It was not their fault.

Has anyone seen my Mopser?
A comely dog is he
With hair the colour of Charles V
And teeth like ships at sea.

The Bandog by Walter De La Mare   (1873 – 1956)

Preface

This book is about all the dogs in my life. But dogs are not the only family pet I have cared for. There have been in the distant past, pet mice, a series of goldfish, budgerigars and cordon blues, zebra and waxbill finches. However in Ghana I found both interesting and amazing the abilities of two house pets. I had both an African Grey Parrot and a Lesser Spotted Green nose Guenan Monkey. Both had remarkable intellects and a significant relationship with me and my wife.

The monkey came to us as an orphan found clinging to its dead mother. She had been shot for food. Instantly it took to Jocelyn and became part of our family. It never opened its mouth to receive a piece of fruit. Instead fruit was always handed to it and Jackie turned it over to inspect it before placing it in his mouth. He savoured his food. He was inquisitive. I drove with him on my shoulder. I walked with Jackie down to the Tema harbour where we sometimes took a walk along the high wall. He accompanied me wherever I went. If he detected danger, he leapt up into my arms. The bond was strong. At that time Jackie was our one and only child.

But I had another pet. Kofi, an African Grey Parrot. I lived at the Kortu Gon compound in Tema, twenty-two miles east along the coast from the country's capital at Accra. He lived in a strong metal cage kept usually in the front garden but if I was working at home or in the evenings, Kofi came into the house.

He loved to sit on my typewriter and travel up and down the carriage as it set a new line. A bell sounded once, when the carriage was fully extended. Twice, actually. Kofi never missed a trick. He began to speak in English and in Akan Twi as I was now speaking that language. He was hand-trained and stood on one leg to crack open kola nuts.

He sang Lilli Bolero, the BBC World Service theme on the hour each hour and he sang the tuneful Ghanaian National Anthem. He was a quick learner and a keen one too. He was in my mind long after we left him in the safe hands of a Ghanaian friend, Juliana Kailey Nii-Moi, when we left Africa. So much so that I have written a novel featuring him, entitled The Parrot's Tale.

When my wife and I returned to Scotland, I returned to a family home of dogs and that has been my interest since those African days. However in Jackie the monkey and Kofi the African Grey parrot, I was learning more about animal behaviour. I had absorbed their antics, insights and abilities. Now I can put that knowledge into the context of the many dogs I have known in my life. It has given me a greater understanding of each canine breed and left me in wonder at their silent thoughts and deliberate actions.

I am now a volunteer working for the Cinnamon Trust. The National Charity for the elderly, the terminally ill and their pets.

Netherholm
Dumfries.

PART 1
CHILDREN AND PUPPIES

Chapter 1
Nettle and Romance

Marjory Bruce Caldwell née Harvie c 1933.
with her Dalmatian dog, Nettle.

I have rarely been without a dog. That is a surprising fact to me. My father was aloof with dogs. He had suffered many canine confrontations in his parish visitations with Alsatians, Poodles, Boxers, Terriers and latterly Doberman Pinchers, Dogues de Bordeaux and Rottweilers. That had left a mark in his mind. It was not that he disliked dogs; it was that he never got down to their way of thinking to gain their loyalty.

My mother on the other hand loved dogs. As a child there was always a dog in her house and as a teenager she had a Dalmatian. What do they say about giving a dog a bad name? It was indeed called Nettle. It did not sting of course, but it occasionally bit. Today there would be a public outcry leading to a petition fuelled by a hungry press to have a dog put down if it bit anyone. But in those days and in my first fifty years of life, if a dog bit you, you were often told you must have deserved it, asked what you had done to annoy it and of course it was largely your fault that you were bitten. Let sleeping dogs lie, was the sage advice in those days.

Today children bitten by dogs cost US insurance companies $345 million a year, while canine attacks in England are estimated to cost the NHS £3.3 million per year. If there is a breed more distrusted than any other, I maintain it is often the irksome journalist, immoral banker or the misers of the insurance world.

The Dangerous Dogs Act of 1991 nevertheless does address and restrict dangerous dogs, while the disfigurement of dog bite victims, deserve our heartfelt sympathy. Placed in perspective however, it is reassuring that there is only 1 dog in 3.9 million dogs known to kill anyone. You are 573 times more likely to be killed by a car and three times more likely to be killed by lightening than killed by a dog.

The top biting dog was recorded as being the German Shepherd. The English Springer Spaniel was also marked high.[1] I know which dog I'd prefer to have bitten me as I regularly suffer a Springer spaniel's unintentional bite. It's more of a nip but for a child it would be more serious. I have the occasional nip to the chest, leg, stomach or arm and that is only to welcome me as I prepare to take him for a walk!

87% of dog bites are suffered by boys.[2] Meanwhile in the United States no less than three Pit-bull dogs are shot and killed every day because of aggression. But most dogs come into the world to be with a family and be faithful to them.

I came into the life of Glen, a border collie in 1950, the year I was born. So often a dog becomes part of a family. Seen from all dogs' point of view, it is a very different experience to have a child added to the existing family, unlike a family welcoming a new canine member to its fold. The former requires accommodation. The latter requires acceptance.

My father was wife-less, dog-less and practically homeless when he came to Bishopton as a young minister shortly after the end of the Second World War. In this small Renfrewshire village the post was served by Tom Pollock but he had reached retirement. His successor was pretty Nessie Buchan, a young girl of nineteen years of age, who delivered local letters and rode her bicycle to reach farmhouses and rural homes. One day she stopped my father.

'How would you like to have a dog?' she asked with a cheerful expression to the new minister.

It was a cruel, hard question to answer. Dogs had been in his family home but his younger brother knew how to tend to them. He became a vet. To Jim, that family Border terrier was a thing to walk on a lead for some exercise, and some exercise for the dog too.

Jim felt grateful for the proposition, but was he ready to take on this responsible step?

Nessie dared not push the matter too far but she seized the opportunity which the minister's hesitation created.

'There's a litter of beautiful pups. They're collies and they are at the farm at Georgetown.' (Georgetown was only a short bicycle-ride away from the Rossland manse in Bishopton.)

'I'll think about it', he said..... 'I'll let you know tomorrow.'

That evening the minister called on his girl-friend who was soon to be his fiancée. He explained his afternoon meeting and proposition. Marjory immediately displayed a keen interest. Her own cocker spaniel, Patsy, had recently died and while Patsy was really her father's dog she missed the little dog around the house.

'Let's tell Nessie we are interested,' she said.

'Why not cycle to Georgetown and see the litter ourselves?'

So the day was chosen. It was a brisk one in the month of January bringing tears to the eyes of the cyclists as they pedalled through the bitter morning air.

The farmer's wife welcomed them and led them to a shed where, in straw, there lay huddled close to their mother, five or six tiny black and white puppies. It was difficult to make a choice. It was difficult to see where one pup ended and the other one began. Eventually they agreed it would be the smallest of the litter, the frailest last-born that was chosen; not for its weakness but for the evenness of his markings and even more kindly look in his eye and the solemn, almost pitiful expression of hope that he'd be chosen that day.

So without any fuss, he was handed over and at the same time the name 'Glen' was made his chosen name.

'Isn't he adorable,' exclaimed Marjory.

A small payment was made although more was offered. The dog was pure collie bred, but there was no pedigree certificate. That's how it was on the farm where a good home was all that was required for the litter.

The little hairy bundle rode silently in the bicycle basket to Marjory's home where her father brushed and de-matted him. When he was suitably groomed, he was taken to the manse where he settled down immediately on a large black rug before a blazing fire. He was to love that rug to the end of his long happy life but in the meantime, he was lost in the carpet's deep pile; without a trouble in mind.

To begin with he grew quite imperceptibly, just like a baby, but in the Spring when all the plans for his master's wedding were being drawn-up, he had grown out of all recognition from the little pup he had been and had become a very loving, very active, and handsome young animal. When the September wedding arrived, he was almost fully grown.

Glen was a noble beast in his appearance. His coat was mainly black with even white patches. His eyes were brown and kindly. His face, mainly white but with matching black borders. His chest was a broad white apron. In every way he was a balanced creature.

His intellect was almost human, so much so that I am now going to attribute thought and speech to him for the rest of his story; for sometimes I feel there is not much that separates a noble beast from a less than noble human.

Chapter Notes

[1] Reiser I.R. Behaviour Assessment of Child Directed Canine Aggression Injury Prevention Ed13 No 5 2007 (348-50).

[2] Broga in Dog Bites in Children 1995.

Chapter 2
At Home in a New World

Miller, Glen and Joan at Fairlie, Ayrshire 1954.

Coming to live in the manse was the beginning of Glen's new adventures. But Nessie Buchan, the instigator of this canine acquisition, always gave Glen a special welcome when she called to deliver the post. Their bond strengthened each time she called, then one day, Nessie suggested Glen should accompany her on her postal rounds. This arrangement was in no way attributable to the minister and his wife. It was one of those natural inklings of a collie to serve. Marjory did not fear Glen running away but was slightly concerned that Nessie might be taking on an unknown quantity. Nevertheless she agreed the suggestion should be given a trial run.

Glen never strayed from the revolving spokes and sat outside each house to await Nessie deliver her letters. The initial trial was a great success and so Glen began his working life as a postal assistant in Bishopton.   Villagers saw him scurrying along the road home from his postal round; his scraggy little string of a tail wagging from side to side. That tail was to grow thicker and stronger, black with a white tail-light at the end, a handsome tail indeed. He was constantly observant and mystified when Marjory lit a fire in the fireplace of a room to see smoke curling its way up the chimney.

'How clever people are,' he thought.

Glen became familiar with sparse furniture in the rooms; second hand chairs and tables, a large sideboard in the dining room which had once occupied space in a hotel foyer – but he was never allowed to enter the dining room. He knew the places where the door was shut to him. He could however go freely into the sitting room where the second-hand "What Not" with its tiny shelves holding knick-knacks intrigued him.

Sometimes his actions led him back to times thousands of years ago as he turned round several times before lying down. This was him imitating the primitive behaviour when his ancestors trampled down the long grasses to make their beds. Sometimes he lay fast asleep; his limbs twitching as he dreamed perhaps of some adversary of whom he was afraid. But Glen was no coward and he was gentle by nature.

Like all dogs, Glen had his likes and his dislikes. The latter were few in number but first fear by far was The Order of the Bath. It seemed unnatural to be immersed in warm soapy water and be rubbed all over with some soapy substance which sometimes got to his eyes and stung. It was a great relief when the operation was over and he was rubbed down with his own special coarse towel. That however was often too late, for immediately he was set down on the floor, he shook himself so violently that the sprays of water scattered in all directions. He would pause, assess his degree of dryness then give it one last dervish dance. His mournful eyes said it all. This was a disgusting heathen practice he must endure at least a few times a year.

The result was magnificent of course. A brushed Glen after a bath brought out sheen as he lay contentedly and exhausted on his special black rug. So Glen did not enjoy a bath, yet he loved to plunge into the sea or into a less salty river or loch.

The world was a happy place for him. He relished his food and always licked his dish clean, smacking his lips and nosing the empty dish around the linoleum kitchen floor.

Much remained a mystery to him. At first, the year's seasons must have mystified him. But rain, sleet, snow or sun he enjoyed being out with the bonus thought to return to the fireside and black hearth in winter or stretch out on the cool kitchen linoleum in summer. Growing up near Greenock, one of the wettest towns in the UK, meant he took spring and winter floods in his stride for they gave him an opportunity to swim, his favourite exercise in which his master did not indulge, even on holiday. He found summer's cloudless skies rather exhausting but of course he could always retreat indoors to the kitchen whose linoleum covering lay over a stone cold concrete base. The kitchen was his base. Brief forays into the hall or the sitting room marked out his territory but frequently the bottom step of the stairs marked the end of the indoors world for him.

The first floating flakes of a snowfall that hung tantalising in the air before they fell and lighted on his nose, touched him with pleasurable excitement. He saw no menace as the fall got steadier and heavier, and as night fell and his master put up the shutters without any apology, Glen dropped off to sleep and dreamt about the soft white carpet he'd be frolicking in when morning came. He lived for each day and it made Jim and Marjory happy to see the expressions of contentment in his beautiful brown eyes

The only one day in the week he detested was Sunday. There were no letters to deliver with Nessie on that day. Even walks with master and mistress were shorter than on other days. The signal that that day had arrived was the 10am Church bells. It was the call to Sunday school. Glen could hear the chatter of the gathering school children. For him it was to be the day of silence. In the Church hall Jim and Marjory would be talking to the children about something that held no interest for a dog on a manse rug. To make matters worse the bell-rope got pulled again at half past eleven to call the grown-ups to morning service; and this was a much noisier affair for Glen as he could hear the drone of the church organ and the singing of the congregation.

The master and mistress came home for an early lunch but they were gone again for a Bible Class at three in the afternoon. This meant that his first walk would be a short one between lunch and Bible Class and the next one would be after dark. Briefly his owners came back for afternoon tea, but the terrible bell rang again for evening services at six-thirty and when that service ended Glen would not see his master again for he and Marjory went to a meeting called the Youth Fellowship and they never came home again till 10pm. It was a day wasted for a dog. How Glen wished that Sundays were not part of a week.

By Monday morning all was forgiven. Dogs rarely nurse grudges. After all Nessie had five more days of postal deliveries to attend to with Glen. One weekly walk was enjoyed by Glen so much so that he became hot-paw excited as soon as he knew the direction Jim or Marjory would be taking. It was to the monkey-house at Formakin. It was a tree lined walk with much sniffing to attend to but at the venue were the monkeys. It was a rather deceptive description because there were no monkeys, well not real ones. They were stone-made and sat on the roofs of the mansion, without a scent.

On another walk Glen would accompany Jim and Marjory by the back minor Greenock Road to the Viewpoint. They were always keen to take visitors there for the magnificent view over the widening River Clyde to Dumbarton Rock and down river to Gourock and across the Firth to Kirn and Dunoon. A human perspective outshines that of any dog whose four feet on the ground prevent such panoramic views. And of course dogs see in black and white only. But Glen did not mind as long as they did not stay too long at one vista. Smells and sniffs were always more interesting.

In mid-September when they went brambling on the road to Glenshinnoch farm, Glen would sniff round the hedges whilst his elders took pleasure standing around picking berries, putting the plump ones in their mouths with stained fingers and rolling them around their reddened palates.

'Freedom to roam is my birthright,' thought Glen. 'The manse garden is large enough to run in, to chase a ball the master kicks into the weeds, to play hide-and -seek among the potato shaws, to bury my chewed bones in the lanes after the potatoes have been harvested. The field over the garden wall is fine to romp in among the wheat stooks and the corn stacks. The farm nearby is worth investigating too. But such observations was not my purpose in life. 'I am a working collie,' declared Glen.

And work there was for him, apart from his postal duties. When his owners went on holiday they decided Glen should have a break too. So a nearby farm agreed to take care of him during their absence.

Nobody intended that he should be given work to perform but the farmer took him to a field where there were cows to be brought in for milking. He gave Glen firm instructions and he quietly brought the animals home, keeping control; with amazing steadiness.

'A born leader,' said the farmer, 'a natural worker if ever there was one, an' I'm a regular judge of a good collie,' he told Jim on his return from holiday.

Such praise pleased Glen but left him confused. If he was so diligent, why then was he not allowed to climb the stairs?'

There were two occasions when he conducted himself with deliberate disrespect for the rules of Jim and Marjory's home.

The first occasion was one when Jim and Marjory had gone visiting friends at the seaside town of Ayr. (Visiting in 1947 meant a long journey changing buses at Largs as the minister was not to own a car for almost another five years.) They had hoped to return from Ayr in the early evening to take Glen out, for a later than usual walk. But they were delayed and had to catch the last bus home that day.

Meanwhile Glen wondered why he had been left alone hour after hour. 'What a humdrum life', he thought. He began to censure his master and mistress reproachfully. Then there occurred to him, a beautiful idea. He'd do a naughty thing. He'd climb the stairs to the master's study, and see a new part of the manse.

It had been a windy day and the study door was ajar. He slipped into find a room whose walls were lined with bookcases and filled with weighty volumes. 'What's in these books,' he wondered. 'Surely they had stories to tell?'

Glen walked around the room straining his neck at the high bookcases. 'I am just a dog,' he exclaimed, wringing a paw in exasperation. But there are compensations. I don't have worries; or a master's furrowed brow, I don't have people to visit, go to hospitals reeking of disinfectant, attend dull meetings or write dull sermons. Yet it would be good if I could write a story one day,' he thought.

It would not be easy. He'd have to sit down quietly and think, think, think. He'd have to have peace and quiet, no disturbances and no interruptions. And it had to be original. Not commonplace; not about hiding bones and going walkies and sniffing delightful smells. Every common or garden dog did these things. It would have to be a brilliant story, a composition about bringing in the cows and driving sheep, helping children and minding babies and doing all the out-of-door things that a collie was meant to do. He hoped when the book was finished, he'd earn a large sum of money and it did not take him very long to decide just what to spend the earned money on. The minister would have his first car. That would mean he'd get round his parish quicker. That meant more time devoted to me and my walks. It would also mean seeing more of the human and rural world.

With these mighty thoughts in his mind, he was aware that the window was slightly ajar. A blast of wind had found this crevice in the window frame and had whisked over the minister's desk, whipping some of Sunday's sermon pages which were now scattered on the floor. Glen poured over the meaningless sheets; then came to the conclusion that they weren't worth reading. It all seemed such nonsense. But there came to mind in his jumbled thoughts an expression he once heard his master utter, when speaking about a man who hopped around Sunday by Sunday from one church to another; from one denomination to another. Jim had called him a sermon-taster."

'Ah', said Glen to himself, 'here's my chance. I can be a sermon taster too.'

He approached one of the sheets now on the floor, seized the corner of it and tore it. He started to chew it. It was not pleasant to the tongue so, sadly he spat it out thinking that sermon tasting was such nonsense.

Jim and Marjory lived in that manse in Renfrewshire for six and a half years. With a paw on his heart, Jim recalled that there was only one other occasion Glen chose to be of dubious service upstairs.

It was when Marjory without any word of complaint took to her bed one Monday morning after breakfast. There had been a bit of excitement the previous day. Her parents had come to visit. Her father was making a fuss of her, but her mother was cool, calm and collected. Jim was making a big effort not to appear too excited. Clearly something was afoot. Someone telephoned the district nurse but not the doctor. The family doctor had recently died and no successor had been appointed. Instead a young doctor from Glasgow each day attended to the patients whose names he had on a list. The doctor arrived daily in the village at 9am. Jim had met him on several occasions.

That Monday morning Marjory's parents arrived early, just after 7 o'clock. That had never happened before. Jim was up and dressed and that was unusual at that time too. Marjory's father left before 8 o'clock in time to be at his shipping office in Glasgow.

In the large front bedroom were my mistress, her mother and the district nurse who had just arrived. Jim and I were downstairs and listening for something unusual but I wasn't quite sure what. Then I heard someone come out of the bedroom. It was Marjory's mother. The nurse had held the bedroom door open for her and like a flash I was upstairs slipping unnoticed through the open door. Nor did they noticed me as I slipped under the bed and lay there quietly panting and eager to know what was happening.

It was all over before I realised it. There was a new sound coming from in the bed. I crawled out from underneath.

Out popped baby Joan. Up popped Glen on to the bed and licked her face clear of mucus. His final instinctive act was to swallow the nutritious after-birth. And so Joan was brought into this world by a mother and nursing collie. This experience did not make Joan a particular dog lover. She seemed to have my father's genes and no dog ever entered her marital home in Surbiton, where she now resides.

The nurse tried to shoo Glen away and scold him in the process after returning to the birthing scene but Marjory informed her that there wasn't a bad bone in his canine body. He was doing what came naturally to him.

Chapter 3
WHEELS

'Wheels,' thought Glen, 'wheels are the very curse of dogs.'

It had been a land of freedom. Marjory and Jim would walk him by peaceful Chestnut Avenue to the riverbank and he could frisk about there, plunging into the river to retrieve sticks thrown in the water by the minister. The way to Chestnut Avenue however was by the main Greenock road on which the wheels of buses, lorries and cars rolled by speedily, charging on and threatening disaster. Glen had seen terrible sights, cats killed and dogs mutilated. Some now with only three legs to move around. Consequently he was always walked on a lead along the main road.

The arrival of baby Joan brought a difference to Glen's life. There were more walks and that seemed a good thing. They were mainly with Marjory. But her walking was more restricted as she guided a pram on all walks. This baby had to have fresh air. But the bumpy roadway of Chestnut Avenue was not suitable for a pram; so all walks were on the pavement now. There Marjory met friends and often there were long conversations on the street. Glen could not wander away for he was never unleashed since the pram arrived. Moreover when the walking resumed, the wheels of the pram were so close to his legs that the occasional accidental collision occurred causing Glen to yelp.

The baby grew but not as fast as pups. It took no less than a year before Joan walked. They were proud of her achievement, overjoyed in fact at the sight of her progress. 'If only Joan was a collie too, she'd be running at that age,' thought Glen.

No sooner was this baby walking that within another six months she acquired a tricycle, and that made life even more difficult. Wheels again. She dashed about everywhere on the back lawn, for she was becoming a natural athlete but she heeded not who might be in the way. She did not hear Glen's cries when she struck him. He had to learn self-defence and dodge out of her path of destruction if he was not going to be injured.

Then came a change of scene. Marjory was no longer taking Glen for walks so he began to think to himself. 'She is going to that place Glasgow a lot. There must be something afoot. When Jim comes back from a meeting or a round of visitation he takes me for walks in the country or by the river. He seems to enjoy my company, but he's no longer care-free. We're not as attached to each other as we used to be.'

When Marjory returned from the city she never told anyone where she'd been but Glen was certainly not a dumb animal. He could see her figure wasn't as flat as it used to be. He guessed that another baby was on its way. And he was right.

It was a boy this time. When Marjory and her new son returned home, it was soon obvious that the child, now named Miller, was not well. He was indeed a very sick baby. Glen did not understand his condition but when his grandparents arrived to look after them all, 'no-one, but no-one' said Glen to himself, 'no-one seems to think of me. They sit up all night nursing the baby. I am no longer given the respect I have become used to.'

But these were unworthy thoughts, for all animals too will forget all else if their young are sick. Soon Miller was taken back to Glasgow. Glen wondered if he was being taken back because he was an unsuitable present, but it was to the Royal Yorkhill Hospital for Sick Children he was taken and there he had a life-saving operation.

Then he was brought back to the manse and everyone was much happier. At last Miller was putting on weight and Glen was brought back to earth. The boy grew strong and plump and no doctor ever had to enter the manse again; apart from socially visiting doctors. Jim's brother Stanley and Marjory's cousin Lala were both doctors and both were pleased with Miller's recovery from infantile hypertrophic pyloric stenosis. So the pram was brought into use again but Glen remembered how to avoid its wheels.

Two years later, without Glen knowing anything about it, a change in fortunes occurred. He never could have imagined he was to move more than a hundred miles away.

'I don't want to go,' seemed to be his expression of disappointment as he sulked beneath the table.

Preparations were made for the great transformation – the move from the green fields of Renfrewshire to Kirriemuir in Angus in the foothills of the Grampians mountains.

Glen saw there was to be no wriggling out of it and in spite of sour depressed looks, the arrangements went ahead for the removal. It was humiliating to be in the thick of it. The removal men with their aprons flying strode into all the rooms of the manse and lifted on their broad shoulders awkward loads. They lifted tea-chests, beds and tables as well as packing precious brittle china stuffed with yesterdays screwed up newspapers. They hardly noticed Glen. None spoke or approached Glen throughout this operation until one man accidentally stood on his paw as he left the manse with a large box. Glen yelped in a moment's pain. This made the man place his box down and approach Glen with words of sympathy. He was a man who must also have a dog. Glen appreciated his concern.

'To think it's all coming true', Glen thought to himself. 'I'm going to miss all my friends, my walks, my cows, my postal round, everything and everybody.' Then a second thought broke through his thinking. 'My master and mistress will be coming with me and the children too. Perhaps there will be new excitement in this new place. After all, I can't do anything about it, so I'll have to make the best of it.'

When the manse stood stark and empty and every footstep heard its echo, Glen felt he'd now be glad to get away and he parted from his first real home with hurt feelings and vague hopes for new ventures. His mistress too had mixed feelings about a new world they were about to enter, but ever practical, she said to Glen as she stroked his head, 'In a couple of hours, we'll be on our way. Our good friends John and Tommy are going to drive us to Kirriemuir.'

The prospect was not attractive for Glen.

'Ride on wheels,' he moaned. 'Ride more than a hundred miles on wheels.' He cowered before the enormity of the terrible ordeal.

The car duly arrived at the desolate Bishopton manse which looked so bare and neglected, stripped of all its furnishings and internal personality.

'Let's all pile in together,' said Jim and so we did. Crouched together the passengers were cosy enough. Curled up on the floor between assorted human legs, Glen found that wheels could be tolerated and even enjoyed as long as they were out of harm's way. And they were on the way from the wet west to the much drier north east.

Chapter 4
KIRRIEMUIR

It was a name that Glen approved of, Kirrie. All proper names he felt should be one of no more than two syllables. Most people who had dogs realised this. Dogs' names should be short and snappy. It might be all right for pedigree dogs to have long handles to their names that make them sound like owners of estates. Glen thought he'd like to meet some of these good-for-nothing gentry' dogs some dark night and have a thundering good fight with them and take the dandies down a peg; but that would be lowering his dignity so that idea had to be dismissed.

'Yes', Glen agreed, 'Kirrie was a good name.'

What he did not know of course was that it was an abbreviation for Kirriemuir and that over the years and centuries there had been other clumsy names pronounced for the town. Kirrie was a town, not a village, and that was a disappointment for a start. The manse was in the very centre of the town. That was a disappointment straight away. Every kind of need was met by shops that were no more than a stone-throw from the manse door. But if Glen were so much as to wander out from the Manse Lane onto the public highway, then something might befall him.

Traffic moved slowly through the Glengate and up St Malcolm's Wynd but the Angus Mill Lorries were cumbersome and heavy and the drivers from their high position at the steering wheel might not notice a collie dog under its weighty wheels.

Next door, over the garden wall was Hunter's garage where the ambulance was kept and, if there was an accident or other medical emergency, the gate was flung open and the ambulance sped away to the scene with sirens blazing to attend to the task of saving life. Had Glen been in the way, anything might have happened to him at such times.

The manse was just over one hundred years old and the church beside it was of an equal age. The manse needed modernisation and it had been agreed that the work should be done before Jim and Marjory took up residence. It was a red sandstone three story house; the bottom floor being the basement. The basement had been entered by a stair-way from the kitchen, but part of the improvement took the form of blocking up the stair-way and making a cupboard at the top of the stairs. The basement was not cut off from the house proper and could be entered now, only from the garden. A flight of steps led down from the front door.

St. Ninian's Manse, Kirriemuir, Angus.

There were other improvements made at the manse preparatory to the family's arrival – a cloakroom with a wash-hand basin off the hall-way; and some alteration to the natty little upstairs bathroom.

The work had not been completed before they arrived so the family were directed to a nearby hotel, an old long-established hostelry where all were made comfortable till they were able to cross the threshold of the manse.

When Jim and Margery came to occupy the house, Glen had a strong and compelling distaste for both house and garden. The entrance shocked him. It compared very unfavourably with the open countryside lane, far from the noise of traffic which led to his previous home. This was a lane too but one that led off a town pavement. The approach was not to a sylvan setting and a wide drive but to a gateway leading to a back garden and thence round the side of the house to the front door. Glen could not understand the back-to-front logic of the Kirrie builder's mind. It was the modest conviction that one must not put ones best features on public display, everything of highest value in the shop window. One had to come round to the private front of the homes to see splendid gardens and staggering views. Some of the plain fronted pavement backs of houses up the Glengate had glorious views over their front gardens, to the Den, the town's public park. The manse too had a view of the end of the Den.

Glen, however, as was noted earlier was not impressed by magnificent scenery. What he particularly wanted was open spaces. Room to run and play and the Kirrie garden lacked that amenity. A path ran in front of the basement and another path at right angles ran alongside a wall separating the manse garden from that of a neighbouring house. The garden was however a steeply sloping one to a gate on Tannage Brae. Kirrie, was indeed, a town of many braes up and down.

A sloping garden gave no scope for a dog to run and play. Moreover, as Glen ruefully observed, complaining bitterly, 'it was as narrow as a hen's face'.

A sandstone wall had been built along the width of the garden with an opening of three steps leading to a level lawn. This wall was open on top for use as a flower-bed, customarily filled with cat-mint. At the extremity of the lawn nearest the steps from the house were two slender graceful birch trees which at suitable times of the day cast their shadows on the lawn. In late autumn they cast their brown diamond leaves on the green grass. Beneath the lawn was an extensive shrubbery of laurel which during Jim and Marjory's incumbency must have hidden in its green inscrutable depth dozens of forgotten tennis balls. Glen was not a retriever as such, more a hoarder.

Below the laurel bank was a solitary plum tree below which the garden ran down to the boundary wall of Tannage Brae with a metal gate crowned by a Maltese Cross at the end of a sloping garden path. And that was all; a small enough garden to keep, but a difficult one. The mulching, digging and planting only led to a limited crop of potatoes. It was hardly surprising that Glen was disappointed; more than half of his doggie life-time having been spent in spacious garden territory. He felt strongly mocked. 'I don't seem able to escape from this confinement,' Glen muttered with painful resignation.

One day, about a week after they had settled in, Jim spoke calmly to his faithfully collie in his study. 'I know it's hard for you to accept the restrictions of this new house and garden. But there's a surprising and glorious variety of pleasure to be found in this quaint town and its surroundings. I'm going to take you on a tour you'll never forget, a walkie that will captivate you forever.'

When Jim came on his own to Kirriemuir for the very first time, to explore the possibilities of settling and working in the Angus town, he was taken by a retired tailor, Ed Watson, on an excursion to sample the magic of the immediate area.

'Glen, I'm going to lead you where I was led. You'll have the freedom of open spaces and I'll have all the attractions of this historic town and of sight-seeing in unspoiled countryside. So let's get on our way. Here's your lead, for we are going to visit the town first and then it will be the attractions of the country walks, where I'll let you run lead-free. Come on. Let's go. Walkies.'

Glen was led from the back door, past the little square drying-green and coal shed to the solid oak entrance gate and into Church Lane. They crossed the Glengate into St Malcolm's Wynd where, on the right stood a house which was entered by outside stairs. They passed the Airlie Arms Hotel, so recently their temporary abode, and came to cross-roads; on the right the narrow Roods with the children's popular Star Rock shop on the corner, on the left the long steep roadway of the Roods, where it was said if you started a rumour at the top, it would have reached the bottom of the street before you could arrive in a fast car.

On they went along Reform Street, the Post Office and Police station on the right with the Reform Street Primary School on the left where the manse brains would start their education.

Glen thought the walk tedious being at the end of a lead but could not communicate his feelings. They proceeded into Bank Street by the ancient Town House to Bellies' Brae after a diversion into Kirk-Wynd via Cat's Close. Up the brae they walked to the Window in Thrums before unwinding their way back home.

But they didn't stop at the manse. They continued down Tannage Brae a few yards further and turned right onto a pink path by a clear running burn - the Gairie. Here I was eventually let off the lead and I pranced about Jim to show my appreciation.

Glen's eyes wandered up the steep slopes that enclosed that beautiful public park in the centre of the town and I scampered about restless and excited. But Jim said there was still a lot more to see, another day.

Tomorrow we will climb another hill and come to the Camera Obscura and watch the changing scenes; the town below, the Airlie memorial on Tulloch Hill, Glen Clova that holds in its grasp the mysterious mountain loch called Loch Brandy. Perhaps one day we'll climb Catlaw together, the nearest peak off the Grampians from Kirrie and on a clear day we can spot Ben Lawyers and Schiehallion.

'Sadly Glen, I have to tell you all this because you are not allowed to enter the Camera Obscura. People don't recognise your special gifts. You're not a harum-scarum little good-for-nothing cratur. You are an intelligent dog but I can't tell that to everybody.'

I also told him I was perfectly happy with him and I didn't want him to be any other way. Except I did not tell him in words, but with understanding looks instead.

We travelled up to the Caddam woods, of famed accordion melody, where we followed a path dotted with many coloured toadstools and came out to the road opposite Kirrie Golf Course.

Neither of us played golf. My master had played this silly game at one time and I had seen his bag of wooden clubs he used as a boy. He told me they were called Hickory woods. But I thought it was a shame to spoil a long walk by pulling a bag of clubs along and worry if you struck a ball with a club and it didn't go in the direction of a particular little hole. People seem to do daft things and I shouldn't blame them for their follies. In this matter of golf, it is played far away from houses in the open air. It is a minor irritation, not like music which is an indoor dreadful affliction,' thought Glen.

Their walk had lasted an hour and a half. Ed Watson had told Jim of the wondrous scenery in the glens which radiated from Kirriemuir to be explored when, one day, he would have a car. Meantime the family moved by Shank's Pony or the buses. Jim did have a bicycle which could be used for visitation in the west-muir which was comparatively flat but most roads were too steep for cycling in this hilly Angus town.

'Back already?' asked Marjory who knew the distance we had planned to go. It wasn't that she didn't welcome us. She was always happy when the minister returned home, be his absence long or short, and in her heart of hearts she loved Glen too and considered, since she always fed him and often walked him too, that he was really her dog.

Chapter 5
Happenings in Thrums

Kirriemuir is known to thousands as Thrums. The noted Scottish playwright Sir James M Barrie, a native of the town gave it that title. Kirrie was a town of weavers and thrums. Thrums were the threads used to repair broken threads in the loom. Kirrie (or if you prefer Thrums) was still a weavers town when Jim and Marjory arrived in 1952. An early morning hooter woke the sleeping town, calling weavers to their machines in the factories. Glen blinked his eyes open at the sound of the hooter then complacently curled himself up again in his basket. Hooters were not for manse folk or manse dogs, he rightly deduced. Rising was less stressed for Glen. He would rouse himself long after the hooter and hurried to make for his water bowl in the kitchen to slake his thirst, and then have a peep and pee out the back door to survey the morning and stake his ownership of the land.

In spring and summertime the weather was usually mild to warm, and being an active dog with a sense of responsibility he looked for something helpful to do. Joan and Miller were still small children. Just how long would it take for them to grow up thought Glen. Joan was nearly five years of age. (mid-life that was for a dog) and she hadn't started to be trained yet. For training, she would soon go to the school in Reform Street but till then she was free to enjoy herself in every possible way. Miller was still under three years of age; at that age, I was fully grown, realised Glen.

The foot of the manse garden was only several yards from the entrance to the Den, and Glen got into the habit of taking the children for a walk on the pink path by the burn. People looked at the scene in astonishment. Some were scandalised but they soon accepted the customary presence of the oddly assorted party. They had to appreciate that there was nothing frightening in this appearance. It wasn't even risky. This dog had a sense of duty. Glen was quite unlike Jim's medical brother who one autumn day took the children for a walk in the den. They were sailing fallen leaves down the burn, pretending they were little boats. Absent-mindedly the doctor turned his back on the children and Miller over balanced and fell head-long into the Gairie. The water wasn't deep but it was muddy at the bottom. The little fellow disappeared beneath the water but he was quickly snatched up by his guilty uncle. The first Jim and Marjory knew of the incident was when they heard Miller's screams as with tears welling from his eyes, he was held by his uncle, who brought him home with a finger-tip grip and a facial expression denoting disgust, for Miller was caked with pungent mud from top to bottom.

If there was something of which Thrums was inordinately proud, it was its Fire Brigade. A new Fire Station had been recently opened in the Glengate. A short distance from the manse. The children, when both of school age, used to rush to the Fire Station at the first piercing sound of the siren to await the appearance and departure of the Fire Engine, usually heading to some farm steading in the country around the town. On one memorable occasion it sped to the haberdashery shop in the town square where a seamstress's distraction had prolonged a hot iron on material, thus setting the shop ablaze.

The firemen were non-professional volunteers who flung themselves on bicycles and struggled hastily into their uniforms en-route, sometimes adjusting belts or helmets as the fire-engine swept away speedily to the conflagration. The departure was a colourful spectacle to watch, but it lasted only moments. When the engine had departed to its destination, all was suddenly quiet and the Glengate returned to its normal sedate condition. The children returned to the manse twice as slowly as they left it, their excitement over.

What we did not realise at the time was that records for turn-out of firemen were being regularly recorded in the county. The record times of fire engine responses by the amateur Brigade which was in rural Angus, the back-bone of the service, was noted with pride.

Jim's need for a car became a priority, especially as his Parish included being chaplain to outlying schools at Padanarm, Kinordy, Glen Clova and Tannadice. It was visiting one particular primary school by bus that the situation came to a head. After speaking to the different classes, he then had a cup of coffee with the school mistress, Miss Jeffries, after which he went over to the school house to spend the rest of the day with the school mistress's very old mother. It was a pleasant pastoral call once a fortnight and the minister had no fault to find with this arrangement. School dinners were provided for the elderly lady and for Jim as well. After four o'clock in the afternoon, a country bus took Jim back home. Miss Jeffries however felt this was waste of the minister's time. She suggested Jim should get himself a car and prepare himself for a driving lesson.

Jim had no mechanical knowledge and was neither willing to learn to drive nor spend any money, which at any rate he did not possess, on a car. But he proved to be an apt pupil studying the highway code from a driver's perception and he was soon ready to sit a driving test. The test was taken in the town of nearby Forfar. To his surprise and that of both Glen and Marjory, he passed first time.

There was no need for further driving lessons in Miss Jeffries car but she said she had a lovely kitten which she would like to offer to the folk of the manse. Jim wasn't very keen to accept the kind offer. Knowing that dogs and cats usually loathed each other, dogs barking and cats hissing, he had some sympathy for Glen. He viewed the prospect of a cat in the manse somewhat apprehensively.

Then came that evening when Miss Jeffries arrived at the back door. It was a cold night setting to rain when she entered and Glen saw under the collar of Miss Jeffries warm coat, was a little furry ginger ball; purring loudly as it was brought into the comforting warmth of the kitchen. There was an attraction about the little creature that Jim and Marjory could not resist.

And so this cat called Trixie took up residence with us. I had no difficulty accepting it. Partly because it was so inferior to myself and partly because I rarely saw it. It was what Jim called a mouser. It lived most of the day outside, down by the Den, seeking out moles and voles, mice and when Trixie was older, rats. You may wonder how I know this. Each morning Trixie would appear at the back door with one or other of these creatures in its mouth. Before entering it would deposit the tailed rodent for Margery to dispose of. It was as if the evidence it brought home was to show how well it had done. I saw from Marjory's expression that she did not need this daily aggravation.

One day the telephone rang in the hall. I was not particularly fond of its high pitched sound but fortunately when people were at home, they approached it promptly and it soon stopped ringing. Jim began speaking to someone who had some very exciting news.

The gentleman on the other end of the line had spent long years of service in India where his work had something to do with the Jute industry. In his spare time he played golf in India. Now he was thinking of giving up both driving and

golf. One could say in frivolity, he was giving up two kinds
of driving.

He had a car to sell and he had golf clubs for sale. Both
were ideal purchases for the minister. The car was an Austin
Ten. A black four door model. It had been an export model
and had quality refinements not available in the home market.
The golf clubs were steel shafted with heads on the "woods"
of some other metal that would not be affected by the heat
in India. But what was of much more interest and utmost
importance was the fact that the clubs were left-handed; just
what Jim was too. It was an opportunity not to be missed and
so a deal was struck.

The golf clubs with bag, some tees and golf balls
became my master's property. He joined Kirrie Golf Club
delightfully situated on Kirrie hill and, while he was an
indifferent golfer, he enjoyed the spectacular views from that
splendid golf-course.

That car was worth every penny that was paid for it and
more. It never let the family down, its courage doubtful only
once, when the radiator got overheated as, with a full car
load of passengers, it was about to tackle the Cairn o' Mount
en route for the Braemar Gathering.

Trixie was not allowed to come with us when as a
family I'd sit in their Austin Ten ESR 117 and we'd picnic
in the Glens or at the seaside at Arbroath. New walks each
time, new sniffs and on each occasion we travelled by car. I
loved being in the back beneath Miller and Joan's swinging
legs. This car took me on many family trips. When I saw the
picnic basket being prepared I was excited. I made sure I was
not forgotten.

How could one find words to tell of the trips to the
nearby Angus Glens? At four o'clock on week days, in
school summer term, the car would be ready at the school
gates, master and mistress aboard with Glen in the rear, to
receive the children for a run to Clova's hill or Prosen's
birches, to Lintrathen Loch with its May profusion of red

rhododendron at the roadside, to pastoral Glen Isla, and, just a little further from home, Glen Esk. Each glen has its own distinctive character, and whichever was the choice of the day there was always a fresh clear stream by whose banks we had our picnic tea and I had time to lap the fresh water.

After Miller and Joan started school, I usually accompanied Marjory as she visited many shops. The bakers were a daily visit and I loved the smell of warm bread. We visited another shop which had greater interest for me. We did not go there every day. I wished we did. It was the Butcher in the centre of town. He gave me a large knuckle of cow bone and I sat for hours on the back garden lawn gnawing away at it. The butcher seemed to like me so much and suggested one day that I take the wicker basket home with the meat inside.

'He's a clever dog, Mrs Caldwell. These collies you can trust. Why don't you send him for the shopping here?'

I saw Marjory study the butcher's face then look at me. What were they thinking?

Two days later Marjory prepared her purse. She checked the amount in it and secreted a piece of paper inside the brown leather folds and placed it in the basket. She then opened the back door and gave me the wicker basket.

'Go to the butcher's shop,' Marjory asked me. So I walked out of the garden and along the pavement till I was opposite the butcher's shop. I crossed the road when all was clear and entered.

The butcher did not see me at first. I placed the basket on the sawdust scattered floor and gave one loud bark.

'Ah it's Glen. Come here my friend.' The butcher began patting my back then with both hands, rubbed my ears. He took the purse from the basket and opened it.'

'Ahh, here it is. Mince today', he said talking some coins from the purse.

He weighted the meat then wrapped it up once with tracing paper, then twice with brown paper tied up with string.

Then he brought another knuckle of bone and wrapped it up too and placed it in the basket. The purse was returned to the basket after the finances had been addressed.

'Straight home Glen. Off you go and don't open the bone till you're home!'

Marjory was delighted with Glen's service and word got around quickly about the minister's dog and his shopping abilities.

Jim did not read a paper every day but on Fridays he never missed reading the local Kirrie Herald and on Saturdays he always bought the national Glasgow Herald. The newsagents knew exactly which paper went to each customer and asked Marjory if she would send Glen to collect the papers too, on Fridays and Saturdays. They had seen Glen shop at the butchers and this would be another talking point in the inquisitive town.

I was delighted to be asked to collect the papers. At first they placed the papers in the wicker basket but sometimes I went without the basket and then the newspapers were rolled up with a band of brown paper in the middle so I could carry them home in my mouth. For as long as I stayed in Kirrie, I had my shopping chores to attend to at the butcher and the newsagents. I loved shopping.

Sometimes the car had far to go. Marjory's mother now lived in the seaside village of Farlie on the Ayrshire coast and when the family went there, the car was full of luggage, despite a leather trunk being sent in advance by British Road and Rail Services. It was always a tight squeeze but it was exciting and the children did not stop talking when we set out.

Visits to Fairlie were either mid-winter when we'd stay only for a few days in the coldness or in the warm sunny weeks when we often went for much longer. This was a winter visit. It was New Year's Day. It grew dark early. We left mid-afternoon with the sky becoming greyer by the minute.

The car headed for Perth via Alyth and Blairgowrie for the route was quiet as we passed the natural unspoiled scenery of the route. By some freak of nature Miller had to stop and visit some bushes at the same spot outside Bridge of Allan every time we passed by and I joined him, just to mark that I had been there too.

The journey was uninteresting and dull for Glen. No dogs to see; no people with dogs, frankly the only comfort came from the warmth of the car engine beneath him and the space he had managed to curl into.

There was hardly a car on the road. The towns and villages were empty. There was little to comment on until we reached Gourock. That was when the children woke up and noticed men staggering about; some falling; others swaying back and forward while crossing the road. The children chuckled at seeing such drunkenness in the open streets. It was just as well there were not many cars around in those days. There were taxis and buses though and from time to time drunk men were knocked down or befell other injuries as they negotiated the streets in their soporific, alcohol-consumed condition.

'Look Glen, see that drunk man?' asked Miller.

'Why should I,' thought Glen. 'Doesn't it make you ashamed of people? You don't find dogs acting like that. I mean, do you? You may find dirty dogs and daft dogs, dim dogs and dignified dogs. You may even find diabolic dogs, but never drunk dogs.'

Late at night they reached Fairlie. I was allowed to run around the garden before a short, lead-collared walk up Southannan Road before sleep in Marjory's previous dog's basket. I slept as soundly as Jim and Marjory but the children kept up the excitement playing with their Christmas presents. With a poor weather forecast due, we set off back to Kirrie after what may have been only three or four days but it had been a busy time as there were other relatives in the village and I was taken to meet all of them. Some of them had cats and were worried how I might react with theirs. They should have had no fears. I ignore Trixie and he ignores me.

Glen did not have an enemy in the world but there were two men in the town that did not really trust him. One was the regular postman. He was a man who had been accustomed to taking risks. He had a distinguished war service. He was one of six Kirriemarians who had won the bravest of medals, the Victoria Cross, over the last century. However he was greeted by loud even angry barking if Glen was in the garden when he delivered the mail. One day when Glen was indoors the postman called and rang the front door bell. 'I must warn you,' he said, 'that I shall not deliver your mail if that dog is in the garden.'

To the manse family this seemed to be a quite preposterous threat. That a war hero should be fearful of Glen was a ridiculous suggestion, but the promise given that Glen would be kept indoors around delivery times was kept. Glen of course would not have harmed anyone although when he barked, he seemed like a very large dog indeed. What is the saying; that a dog's bark is worse than his bite? How true. Glen never bit anyone.

But Glen did have a certain prejudice based on a happy memory. A postman he believed should not be a man at all. The post person should be like Nessie Buchan. The postie should wear a skirt and offer to take Glen on her rounds. But such information never came the Kirrie postman's way.

The other man, who did not trust Glen, lived up at Knowehead not far from the manse though up one of Kirrie's steep braes. This man had a dog too. To be precise it was a bitch and at certain seasons, Glen had a longing. At such times Glen would slip out of the house unseen and make his way to Knowehead. He would sit at the lady-dog's gate, sometimes for hours and he couldn't understand why her master would not open his gate and let him in. Glen was curious and he was patient. Probably the householder was watching television, the new and rare, home-viewing box. Eventually he would get up and go out with his dog. But as soon as he encountered Glen, he retreated to his home and immediately telephoned the manse.

'Come up here at once to Knowehead and take your dog home. He's been sitting at my gate for hours.'

So Marjory climbed the hill and brought the guilt-ridden naughty dog home. These were two men without friendly feelings for Glen. But no one could describe them as enemies.

Glen did have enemies however, and they had taken up residence in the manse. The first indication of their presence was in the kitchen cupboard at the top of the basement stairs. One night the minister was at a meeting and his wife was sitting knitting in the kitchen. She had the wireless set switched on low. Suddenly there was a rattling of some empty jam jars in the cupboard. The rattling ceased for some time and then it repeated its eerie movements. Marjory was not alone.

There were later occasions when the noise returned and Marjory took to sitting in the kitchen with a stout walking stick in her hand. Glen sat in the kitchen trembling and then petrified by the anticipated confrontation of an unseen foe. He could not identify his adversary. It was a new sound. Then one night a strange noise was rising from the dining room. Jim and Marjory rose from their bed to go and investigate. There on the side-board was the fruit bowl with some of the fruit disturbed and by the skirting board lay a banana, half eaten.

On hearing about this, the Kirk Session decided to send in the rat-catcher. With Kirrie's up-and-down hills, the Gairlie stream and nearby farms, it may well be the start of a rat invasion, thought the committee.

Jim and I accompanied the rat-catcher into the basement. I could sense intruders but none were seen. However the rat-catcher left a quantity of Warfarin asking Jim to place the deadly powder at the corners and behind any pots and to leave the basement alone for at least two days before going down to inspect and identify any unwelcome guests.

There was something in the air I detected. It was an excited expectation as the forty eight hours elapsed. Then we returned.

Jim, Marjory and I entered cautiously. My tail was between my legs. Jim said all three of us entered with pounding, throbbing hearts. There was evidence a-plenty but at first we could hardly distinguish between dead rats and potatoes. The mystery was solved. Jim said that we did not need the Pied Piper of Hamelin after all. But even after two days, we were still collecting dead rats.

Not long afterwards, Margery was restless one night. I sensed that it was time for another baby in the house and I was indeed right. Jim got dressed straight away and went out. He roused his next door neighbour who ran the ambulance service and suddenly Marjory was gone and so was Jim. I made sure Miller and Joan were sound asleep and they were. I heard the ambulance return an hour later and Jim returned to the manse. I gave him a welcome to show all was well at home but he did not go to bed. He started to speak on the telephone. Then the telephone rang. A big smile came across his face.

'Are you saying ...it's a boy... and mother and son are doing well? Oh thank you for telling me. Thank you. Goodnight.'

So now there were three children, Joan, Miller and Bruce as they called the new baby. It was a very happy time. The family was complete and I could see everyone was content with life. Grandparents visited to see this new baby and many made a fuss of me too.

It was the month of May and Bruce lay in his pram on the front lawn every afternoon. I saw it as my duty to keep him safe so guarded his pram from any harm.

That was when I began to feel pain. At first it was a sharp pain that went away gradually. Then the pangs of pain increased. I had to lie down, out of harm's way. I was going to lie down in the laurel bush so I could rest away from prying eyes but I did not make it. I collapsed in a bed of flowers.

I don't know how long I had been there but a vet arrived and examined my stomach.

'It's strangulation,' he said. 'I'm afraid I can't do anything here. I'll have to take him to Dundee for an operation.'

'Is he going to die?' asked Miller. That made Joan cry.

'No, I don't think so,' said the vet with an air of assurance.

I remember being driven away without any member of the family. I was in the vet's van for more than an hour until we arrived at an animal clinic. I could hear other dogs in the building but they didn't bother me and I was feeling very sleepy.

Two days later I heard Jim's voice. I knew then that I'd be going home to Kirrie. They made such a fuss of me when I got there and everyone gently patted my tummy where some thread still covered my skin. The next day the vet came to see me and with a pair of scissors, cut away the thread. By then I knew the operation was successful and I began to eat normally and I played with the children in the garden once more. With my recovery complete and the family healthy and growing, I could not have been a happier dog, although I did not run just as quickly as I once was able.

A kindly couple came to the manse one afternoon with a box. They placed Trixie inside. Perhaps Trixie was heading to the animal clinic too but then I learned it found a new home on a farm on the north side of the town.

Larger boxes began to gather in all the rooms and I saw

signs that the family were on the move again. But the older I became, more worry lingered in my mind. Would they find a box for me and will I go to some farm too, just like Trixie?

Chapter 6
Off to Glasgow

Glasgow was calf country for the minister for he had been born just a dozen miles away at Uddingston while his wife had been born in the city itself at Ibrox. The feeling I got was that they were returning home, rather like a dog likes to go back to its origins at the end of its life.

I was surprised how peaceful, verdant and wide streeted Newlands in Glasgow was. The manse was certainly in need of some attention but the Summerfield family joiners who were members of our new church at Shawlands Old Parish Church soon got the manse spruced up for the family.

The second world war air-raid shelter was an attraction and an army helmet was found in the scullery. So too a set of battery field signals with a metal spike to insert into the ground to send Morse codes and flicker replies. I tried to understand Miller's excitement with his new toys. A lick of paint covered the window sashed and permeated the nostrils. A hatch was constructed between the kitchen and the dining room and a door was added to the scullery area where the coal was kept. It arrived through a shoot from the wall outside.

I overheard Jim tell his wife that had they known how quiet the roads were in Newlands, they might not have given Trixie away. Surprisingly Newlands was quieter than Kirriemuir. This was because very early in the morning, those with cars disappeared into the city. Others walked west to Kilmarnock Road to get a city bound bus or they walked the other way to get a blue-circle inner or outer train to the suburbs or centre of Glasgow.

Jim put the age-old question to me. 'Would you like to go back to Kirrie?'

'Not any more. I'm staying here with you,' I replied.

Glasgow's new experiences came to us in an atmosphere which was most congenial for a dog. There were spacious parks nearby in every direction. Newlands Park was very close indeed of course as that was where the manse was, while Queen's Park had a summer band-stand attracting brass bands and family audiences with many dogs besides. Linn Park became a favourite for me with its woodland and river walks but the best and most interesting walks were a car ride away at Rouken Glen. There were parts we had to be walked on leads like in the walled garden but by the pond and the waterfall I could run to my heart's content. Glasgow was less hilly than Kirrie, that was for certain.

On the edge of the new Parish was the Pollok Estate. I did not visit it often but I did enjoy the fields of highland cattle with their wide, spread-out horns as they grazed peacefully in the green estate. There were broad grass avenues enclosed between lofty hedges of rhododendrons. In springtime the pathways were bordered by great stretches of bluebell and always and everywhere the park was shaded by mature trees in delightful variety. Deer could suddenly appear bounding from the trees but when they saw me they changed direction and headed for wooded cover.

Jim saw foxes with their cubs sporting in an open green avenue, blissfully unaware of our presence. He told me of seeing rabbits and other species but I could not give chase any longer and they scuttled away to their lairs defensively when they became objects of interest to the curious. This was a place for the four footed. I loved it. I dreamt about it as I slept. I no longer solely dreamt of holidays.

A holiday in July at Elie on the east neuk of Fife had been arranged before the family left Kirrie and they were ready for a break after getting the manse ship-shape and the front and back gardens under control.

So I returned to that confined space in the car I had with Joan's legs now so long that I had to sit under Miller's instead. Bruce was in a cot between them. After an hour I heard that we were entering Stirling and the car slowed down as it went through the town. I understood when a car slowed down and then stopped but no-one got out that it was probably because the car was at traffic lights. I had just had that experience. Then the gears increased from first to second. Before we entered the third gear, I heard and felt a thud at the side of the car. From where I was sitting, I saw an elderly man's face approach the side window then suddenly there was a bang. This upset Jim considerably.

'I've hit him Marjory. I've hit him. I may have killed him.'

The car came to a stop. A passing police car arrived at the scene and an ambulance was called. The policemen took Jim's name and address and made sure he had not been drinking alcohol. That should have been funny for Jim never drank alcohol. The ambulance took the man away on a stretcher to the Stirling Royal Infirmary. Jim asked how the man was but the ambulance man said it was too early to say.

The policeman made yellow chalk marks on the road and then Marjory got my lead and took Joan and Miller for a walk in near-by King's Park while matters were discussed over the accident. Bruce slept on in his car cot. As we left the car, I smelt blood and noticed some was smeared on the very end of the side of the car.

We returned after a good walk to find Jim seated in the car ready to go. He told Marjory that the man had a broken nose and some concussion. He lived in a home for the elderly nearby and he now had their telephone number. He would telephone that night and enquire how he was.

'Will you be going to jail?' asked Miller.

'I'm not sure what the police might do. I asked them and they said they would give their superior a report of the incident. I would hear in due course. But as it's the first time I've been the subject of the police, I hope it might be taken into consideration, if I do go to Court,' said Jim.

The car went silent. I think they all had their own thoughts about what might happen. Only time would tell. But perhaps they needed another break and at Perth not only could they have that but also a visit to Jim's brother, Stanley, to talk through the situation. That was what was needed to calm nerves.

Stanley was a doctor, the Medical Officer of Health for Perthshire and Kinross, and he soon asked about the old man's injuries. He assured Jim, that in his opinion having seen the results of many road injuries, that he was not to blame. He explained that had he struck the victim there would have been leg and body injuries. The fact that it was only blood from his nose indicated that he may have fallen or perhaps tripped and fallen against or onto the side of the moving car.

I was pleased to hear Dr A. Stanley Caldwell say this, as that is how I saw it too. Oh..If only I could talk.

The car resumed and we all arrived at Elie. Once the trucks and cases had been taken in to our holiday home Jim telephoned his friend the minister of Dunblane Cathedral and explained his motoring problem. He agreed to visit the man in Stirling Infirmary and would ring him back when he had done so. He phoned back with more cheerful news. The injury was just a broken nose but interestingly the Home where he came from explained that he often wandered out and into the road where he sought to find cigarette ends. He had just spied one good looking cigarette butt when the accident happened. Furthermore the Home said the incident had been providential in as much as there would now be no more permission for their patient to leave the home's premises without supervision.

There was no prosecution letter on their return home. The matter was soon forgotten by the police, the old man and the children but the face against the window and the thump will remain in my mind and Jim still wonders how it all happened and drives with much caution these days.

The following summer I heard that we were going on holiday to a long sandy beach at the town of Port Stewart in Northern Ireland. That meant crossing from Ardrossan in a large boat. That excited me and the children. Shortly before setting out I collapsed and lay in a heap in the hallway. I knew that it felt like the last time I collapsed in Kirrie and hoped they could repair the damage just as quickly this time. The pain was excruciating and Jim and Marjory knew it. So I was taken by Marjory to a lady vet who was thought of highly.

At her surgery she did not take long to reach her conclusion. She looked into my eyes and put her stethoscope to my heart. Then she gave her verdict. She pronounced my death sentence.

'Neither I nor my husband would agree to that course of action,' said Marjory with a sternness I had never heard her use before.

'Very well,' said the vet, 'he's your dog. I've given my advice.'

Without another word we left the vet's surgery. Marjory spoke very sadly to me. But the pain had eased with this walking movement and I kept up a good pace. A policeman approached and Marjory spoke to him.

'Do you know any vet who could perform an urgent operation on this dog?' she asked.

'That's a difficult question for me,' he said. 'There's a very good vet not far from here. I've had dealings with him and I suppose I'm the last person who should recommend him. He's been in a lot of trouble with the police for drunk-driving and, in fact, at the moment his driving licence has been suspended. But I can tell you he's a good vet. He could be the very man you need.'

Without any further delay we made our way to that vet's surgery. He was a very kind and thoughtful man who examined me with his gentle prodding fingers with much care. 'I think we'll be able to fix this old gentleman all right.'

His words pleased Marjory and his smile put me at ease. Marjory told him that we would be setting off to Ireland the next day. 'Should we delay our departure for a few days?'

'Not at all,' said the vet. 'Enjoy your holiday your dog will be fine with me and in top form when you come back. Glen needs a rest, not a holiday. I've got time to walk him,' he said recalling his current legal situation. 'I can gently walk him each day after his operation. We'll get on fine. Now off you go and enjoy your holiday.'

Two weeks later the family came to collect me and I jumped up on Marjory then Jim and then for longer cuddles from Joan, Miller and Bruce. I was surely a tough old thing after two operations and I knew no vet would ever again think of passing the death sentence as long as I was awake.

The one enclosed place I knew and entered and left every day was the manse. I learned that the house had been left to the Church by a former minister who had owned it. It was a two story red sandstone building with a very large attic above which, had it been divided off, might have contained three bedrooms of a moderate size. The last minister had only one child and no dog, so there was no need for him to make use of this large space.

With three children and a dog it was deemed necessary to build a partition in the attic. Before they moved in, the alterations had been made by Mr Jonny Summerfield, the carpenter/joiner elder.

I was permitted to have full freedom of the house, including the spacious lounge which was at the upper floor level. But I like best to climb the narrow stairs at night and sleep beside Miller and Bruce's beds.

The gardens back and front were level and of moderate size. In the far corner of the back garden Miller played under an iron roof wearing an army helmet. The property still had its air-raid shelter when we arrived. I was allowed in there but it was cold, dark and miserable most months of the year.

Thank goodness it was not decreed as an outside kennel for me. I was glad to see it demolished and in time I inspected the walled compost construction. It seemed that old vegetables and cardboard went in there.

Chapter 7
At Christmas Time

At the darkest time of the year I always noticed the arrival of heavier mail through the letter box. Normally letters were opened and papers read then either binned or retained for action. But when the multitude of cards arrived in December, they were opened, checked to see who had sent them, marked off on a rota sheet and then, they seemed to appear on every open space in the house. On top of bookcases, mantelpieces and side tables they appeared. Even some were hung one after another on a vertical string.

Then one night after the children were sound asleep I followed Jim up to their bedrooms. Jim walked very slowly and did not put the light on. Instead he laid some boxes by the foot of the boys' beds and filled their stockings with apples, nuts and tangerines. Then he did the same for Joan. It seemed a very strange annual custom.

I had seen a feast in the manses only once a year and it was always the same food they ate and shared with me. Roast Turkey and sausages were my favourites. I got them at night, cold. I don't think I would have enjoyed them as much had they been hot. Nor could I have eaten plum pudding, Christmas pies, sprouts or cranberry jelly which everyone else enjoyed.

Another mystifying part of Christmas was when at the table, every one wore different paper hats. They never did this on any other day of the week and they never explained why they had to do it then. But that was only the start of the confusion as explosions erupted which caused them to laugh out loudly as they pulled to snap open these crackers. I did not like that noise and always sought a quieter part of the house when that noise began.

To confuse me still further a tree was brought into the lounge and placed at the front window. Jim made sure it was well balanced but always left Marjory to decorate it with lights and hanging baubles. I sniffed around the tree but no other dog had left a scent and so I though wisely not to imprint mine. I began to think this tree would always be in the house but several days after Christmas, it was taken down and taken outside where this tree should have been all along.

But before that, an even more unusual happening took place that year. One I had not seen before. The lounge was full of relatives with young children and their parents. All patted me as they arrived and I could sense there were not just visitors but family.

Jim left the party mid-afternoon informing all that he had a Christmas duty to be at the Victoria Infirmary nearby where I knew he often visited as its chaplain. But I left the room with him and he did not leave the house. He retired to his bedroom. I slipped in to see what he was up to and he closed the door behind me.

That was when I saw the transformation take place. He attached a long white beard to his face. Then a bright red cloak was worn with a large black belt to keep it in place. He wore a matching red hat with a white furred edge. He opened the wardrobe and produced a large sack. These were very mystical happenings. Then he lifted a bell and held its clanger so as not to make a noise.

This new Jim then opened the door and when all was quiet, he walked down stairs away from the collected merrymakers. I followed him down because I knew underneath all the fancy dress was Jim.

Then he started ringing the bell as he mounted the stairs. 'Ho, Ho, Ho,' he said, but I am not sure to whom.

'Have I arrived at the right house?'

'Hey, it's Santa. Yes, come in to the room Santa.'

The children seemed very happy to see an unrecognised Santa Jim dressed this way. Santa then distributed presents to all the children who approached the bearded man. Each of them politely thanked Santa for their gift. Only one boy saw through the disguise. Brian, who has been blind from birth, received his present.

'Thank you Uncle Jim,' said Brian.

'No Brian, it's not Uncle Jim, its Santa,' said his sister Dorothy. But Brian did not correct himself and I am glad he didn't because both Brian and I knew this was not Santa but Jim dressed up in most peculiar clothing.

Jim returned in his pastoral uniform to learn that he had missed Santa. All the young children told him so.

The lounge fire juggled roaring flames and the older members of the party sat back and prepared themselves for a post-prandial snooze. But their slumber did not last long as Jim sat at his Bechstein piano and played popular tunes. I knew they were so, because many sang to them. Miller joined with a pair of drumsticks hitting the glass coffee table and a sturdy rose budded vase.

The evening of happy insanity ended. I walked through the discarded crackers and paper hats, torn wrapping paper and displaced tinsel. This event only came once a year and I had now seen it more than sixteen times. I lay down by the master's study door. In my weak old age I felt ready to slip into that happy hunting ground, to sleep and never wake.

Chapter 8
In Memoriam

Glen had now lost his voice. For Glen was weak and his faculties were fading. Glen had reached beyond a dog's allotted span. He still enjoyed his food and his shorter daily walks of course but they were getting shorter by the day. He was surely cheating the grim reaper and all our own care for him was merely postponing the final parting. He seemed to be getting smaller too, contracting into something that was more pitiful to look on – a shrivelled body.

The old troubles returned but did not seem to be accompanied by the old searing pain. It was plain it was time to take him back to the kindly vet who had kept him during our holiday in Northern Ireland earlier that summer.

When we arrived at his surgery, we found the door locked and the windows boarded up. The helpful policeman was telephoned. He informed us that he would be with them in a few minutes without any further information. We stood at the bolted door until the officer arrived.

He greeted Jim and Marjory with a handshake.

'I'm sorry I can't help you this time,' he said in a whisper as if not to worry Glen. 'You see, he really went too far this time. He drove his car when his licence was suspended. He had an accident again. Now he's serving his sentence in Perth Prison.'

Jim lifted Glen back into the car and drove him home. A reprieve from execution no one wished. He lay down in the dining room close by the door and gave a fond look, virtually a farewell message of thanks for more than sixteen years of loving care. We knew it was the end.

That night we searched in the telephone directory to find the RSSPCA, the Royal Scottish Society for the Prevention of Cruelty to Animals. They offered to collect Glen the following day around 11am.

The next day would be a school day for the children of course but Miller was privy to Glen's final arrangements. He sat with Glen as he slept; gently massaging his head and back. He had not known any day in his life without this collie. He cried himself to sleep.

The morning was worse for him. As he prepared to leave for school he knew he'd never see him again. When the school bell sounded to announce the morning break it was at 11am. He walked alone in the playground and shed a tear.

'C'mon old chap,' said the kind and gentle RSSPCA officer. You've had a good innings. You're due your rest.'

Marjory and Jim saw him lifted into the van. Some people like to see their beloved pet's life-less body when it's all over. They didn't feel they could face that. After all, for sixteen years Glen had been a lively and faithful companion. We all preferred to remember him like that.

Perhaps Glen would have had for us a quotation from George Borrow as his final message – "Every dog has his day and mine has been a fine one."

Tâche, the middle of three collie pups.

Tâche the puppy in Arbroath 1991

Ben

Blu

Bobby

An ever alert Bobby

Bobby at work for the community.

Buck left; Bobby right

Blu in July

Hilda the Basset Hound with Ernie the Dachshund.

Jim with Tâche the puppy.

Camera shy Tâche

Tâche at Tee 5, Spion Kop

Tâche in Glen Clova

Tâche with his mother.

Dog rescued in the River Nith

Tâche with his cousin Tess

Tâche slowing down

On guard on the stairs

Ziggy Nicolson in summer

PART 2
ADOLESCENCE - FRISKY

Chapter 9
Rock the Wrecker and Ben the Bounder Kirrie the Assassin and Rikki the Rogue

As a sixteen year old, I would not experience a parental dog for some considerable time. Nor would I be able to, as soon as I left home. But there were some childhood memories and encounters left in my mind which deserve some reflection.

Glen had been a source of comfort to each of us especially when matters were not going our way. Glen would sit at my father's fireside hearth when the words of a sermon were not forthcoming. He seemed to sympathise as I learned poetry homework and never complained if my swinging legs under the table kicked him when I was doing my sums. Little did I know then that we are apparently better solving mathematical problems with a pet present.[1] It would be a progressive school indeed to welcome the family dog to sit in the examination room under the pupil's desk. But it might reflect on even better school exam results! I began to think all dogs, if provided with food, love, exercise and security were accepting of our ways; non-judgemental, loving and understanding.

That view was shattered when a bachelor vet uncle from Dumfriesshire appeared with his side-kick, Rock, a border terrier. This was my uncle David, my father's brother, who was a vet in Thornhill in Dumfriesshire. I had been given a pair of sturdy brown leather shoes. I had tried them on. They fitted perfectly. A strong leather scent added to their comfort, and made them very special indeed. I had been warned not to kick a ball or climb trees with these good Sunday shoes.

The unsaid fact was that they must have cost a considerable amount of money for my impoverished parents.

The very next day, on a Sunday morning, I came down for breakfast to find a mangled, distorted leather shoe, ripped with Border terrier teeth marks, the sole evidence of the destruction. I feared receiving the blame for not having removed the temptation from the teeth of the wee dog by placing them out of reach. But I was only six years old at the time and such a contemplative act of shoe protection was beyond my comprehension.

With hind sight I can now understand what probably went on in Rock's mind. He had come to visit the manse from a bachelor's home. There in Thornhill he knew who the pack leader was. But in this household there were three children, two other adults and a collie. He may have been frightened by the number of people he was encountering or acting like a spoiled terrier but unbeknown to him was my strong feeling of loss. The brown shoes were never seen again and nor were they replaced. I did not have a favourable word for this Border Terrier, Rock the Wrecker.

Our next door neighbours in Newlands were the Linton family. Watson and Joan Linton had two boys, much younger than I was and a beagle. Ben the Beagle was a white-socked chestnut and black- back saddled charmer. My offer to exercise Ben was welcomed and I agreed to walk him on Friday nights and on Saturday afternoons. The only instruction I was given was to keep him on the lead until he was in the park. I assumed that was because he could not be trusted to walk to heel on the busy streets without a lead.

I may have been in the second row of the schools rugby team but nothing prepared me for a dog which was determined to run me off my feet. Beagles are friendly, lively and affectionate. It may be implied that this breed's specific attributes come in equal measure. Maybe they do. But for Ben, I'd say he was 20% affectionate; 20% friendly but 60% lively.

He always gave a strong pull on the lead as if he thought that south-side Newlands Park was closing in twenty minutes. Walking to heel was not for him, no matter how much I tried to restrain him.

When I asked him to be a good boy and then let him off the lead, he ran like a greyhound all around the park borders. His behaviour certainly gave him exercise but he would not respond to my call. It took some time before I let him off the lead after that. However when I decided he had long enough under close supervision, I would release him again. Any and every scent he'd follow, every time. Never did he look back to see where his lead-holding companion might be. Just what was I walking, I wondered as I stood forlorn with an empty lead in my hand? This was a dog that would not Take The Lead.

How different a beagle was to the loyal, eye contacting collie Glen had been. I decided this was becoming a chore which I could do without and so after a few weeks, I gave up on Ben, Ben the Bounder.

On our return from visiting the former manse and its new minister at Kirriemuir, we learned that a dog breeder in the Perthshire village of Alyth had pedigree golden cocker spaniels and we decided to call in to see them on our way home to Glasgow. There was much excitement in the back of the car at the thought of another family dog.

There were two puppies and a proud cocker spaniel mother in a run. One male cocker came to us immediately and we fell in love with it. The deal was done and so it got to know his new family in the back of our tail-winged Austin Cambridge motor car as we continued home to Newlands.

It did not take long to name him. Kirriemuir where I grew up was affectionately referred to as Kirrie and so Kirrie the golden cocker spaniel joined our family.

Quite unlike Glen, Kirrie came with paperwork. It proved his pedigree but we would never be showing him at Crufts let alone any dog show. I sensed Kirrie knew he was a pedigree dog. He had a certain licence to do what he wished at times. On a walk, his behaviour was immaculate. He respectfully passed other dogs by, without too much attention. In an open space he would come to the call when off the lead. But there was another side to Kirrie, a darker canine side.

My first confrontation had mundane beginnings. My mother was seated near the fireside knitting. Her ball of wool rested on her lap. As I passed by, the ball of wool fell on to the carpeted floor. Instinctively I retrieved the wool. But I had not seen Kirrie lurk like a killer shark on the other side of the chair. Suddenly my hand was locked in his mouth clamped by two sharp rows of angry white teeth. Blood dripped and when he eventually let go, several fingers exposed raw bone with the skin in bloody shreds.

Had this been a one off incident, it would have been forgotten in time but Kirrie had sensed blood and more was on his mind.

I had a white rabbit at that time. I knew I must keep them apart. Snowy was in a raised hutch outside in the back garden with an enclosed compartment and an open meshed area where he could observe Kirrie spray his territorial markings in the back garden. One summer Sunday evening, when church services were still held at that hour, my parents were in attendance and my sister played her clarinet in the lounge. I had ensured the side gate was closed in the back garden and released Kirrie for an hour.

After sufficient time elapsed, I opened the back door to let Kirrie in. I instantly saw the hutch wire mesh was torn and bent upwards. To my horror the carcass of Snowy lay on the grass, staining it red. Kirrie wagged his tail to show how good a hunting cocker he was and he was delighted to be returning into the house, job done.

My father called the breeder at Aylth. He had wondered if Kirrie might have been like the other puppy and his canine father. It was confirmed that both were very highly strung, possibly over bred to secure a lengthy muzzle for showing them at meetings, but what Kirrie was not, was a family pet. There were several bitings to report in due course as well as the rabbit killing. Dog lessons had not address his wicked streak. So Kirrie was returned to Aylth from whence he came and we heard no more. Kirrie was a beautiful dog but not such a wonderful dog. There were too many black dog days for this golden cocker spaniel, Kirrie the Assassin.

The blackest dog we ever had was next. It started on a very black day. In fact it was a residential funeral which was taking place in Newlands Road nearby when the widow excused herself from the reception room where the service was taking place. She later apologised to my father somewhat unnecessarily. Her pedigree black poodle had been giving birth during the service. There was something reassuring even celestial in birth arriving at the time of death, as it was for Robert Burns last child, but it led to the widow inviting us to see the two poodle puppies, a few weeks later.

Ministers were never recompensed financially for services rendered whether they be baptisms, weddings, or funerals. With no money exchanging hands, baptisms produced cake; weddings provided parker pens and cake and funerals offered great bunches of chrysanthemums. This sad occasion was most unexpected. This funeral would offer a puppy to the dog-less family.

I lifted up one of the poodle pups. It was hard to distinguish which end was which. These balls of black wool were extremely cute until one end produced a widdle. Then I could address it properly. The widow was more than happy to see one of her pups move a few hundred yards away to Monreith Road and so after a collie, and a cocker spaniel we now had a poodle. Not a Standard but a simple Caniche French poodle. The sophisticated French and the practical Germans both regard the Poodle (Caniche) as their national breed. The British perhaps regard the poodle as the most pretentious popular house dog. Gone are the days when this ancient breed was regarded as a good water-game dog. Rikki (perhaps the popular comedian of the day, Rikki Fulton, had something to do with his naming) was not keen to enter water at the seaside or into one of the many ponds in Glasgow's numerous parks. He settled well initially into the family of five. He had only two mishaps. The first made him a star in my eyes.

I had come from Kirriemuir to live in Glasgow. From a rural idyll in Angus to a busy slick Glasgow where trams, trolleybuses, a local circular train service over land and an underground train service shoogled along at speed. That was the exciting Glasgow I thought I'd come to.

First day at school was a real eye opener however. I claimed that there was no long-division in Kirriemuir but Miss Dick did not accept my excuse. She was a spinster with a tight helmet of deep black hair, a round bloodshot face with very narrow eyes. Too narrow to be healthy I thought. She proceeded to belt me three times without a break, with the famous Lochgelly tawse. It was the first time I would encounter such educational torture and the first of many times I regarded the punishment as totally unjust and excessive. That this should have happened on my very first day of school in Glasgow convinced me that there was a rougher edge to this city. It was one I was not used to, yet.

Following my belting, I was comforted at the morning break by the concern of Leslie Hecht. Our friendship began on an unusual footing. He asked me if I was Jewish. I hesitated. I remembered hearing that Christ was King of the Jews and so I could answer his question after all. I was indeed a Jew, I informed him.

'Then bring your yarmulke on Friday morning.'

'My what?'

'Your school cap will do. Your parents must be reformed Jews,' he informed me. My father was actually the school's chaplain by this time.

I did not like Miss Dick. In fact I hated her and she hated me. The chemistry was explosive. It was at least a mutual feeling but I shared the hate I had for her, with Rikki. I knew after a year of this treatment I could look forward to having the popular Mr Thomas Stewart as my teacher for the year and so the final term summer church service was a real watershed away from the dreaded Miss Dick.

Rikki came into Miss Dick's twisted world in a most unusual manner. As I left the church service in my penultimate year of primary school, I noticed Miss Dick speaking to my father with the charm she left behind when teaching. Two faced indeed. But I gave it no further thought.

That summer I sat in the back of the car with Rikki as we made our hesitant way up the shores of Loch Long and down the shores of Loch Fyne to the sleepy village of Carradale on the Mull of Kintyre. The isle of Arran seemed like a stones' throw away across the Kilbrannan Sound but this was a resort providing coastal and rural walks in perfect picturesque tranquillity which Rikki really enjoyed.

Half way through the holiday my father announced we would as a family and with Rikki, go south to the tip of the Mull of Kintyre to the unimaginatively named village of Southend where Miss Dick was on holiday. She had invited us for afternoon tea.

For the first time in my life, I defied my parent's instruction. On no terms would I enter the family car and visit my adversary, Miss Dick. I informed my sister that I would take my cut-down golf clubs and play the course, round after round on this nine hole course until they returned. My parents could not resolve, understand or manage my stubbornness as it was the first time I had shown this trait and I was pleased and relieved to see them set off, caring little about what retribution I would suffer, almost certainly, on their return.

The darkest of clouds descended on their faces when they returned. I was sent to my bed at 6pm for the night, for my disobedience but I noticed the family's concern was really more about Rikki. My sister informed me of what had happened at Southend that afternoon.

Miss Dick produced afternoon tea together with a plate stacked with seasonal strawberry tarts. She began to pour cups of tea and distribute them. Then she lifted the large round plate of strawberry tarts. But she was in dialogue and the one thing Miss Dick could not do, was two things at the same time. (Apart from belting and screaming in a violent rage towards an unfortunate pupil. Something at which she excelled.)

The plate moved back and forward in her hand as she spoke. The plate moved upwards and sideways as she made her point. It swept low with the crescendo of her story, from where it would not return. The movement had transfixed Rikki's eyes and his finely tuned muzzle got the scent of this seasonal treat. But it was the teasing movement of the plate which excited Rikki. Why should this plate be so active? It was a game he did not enjoy. It was of course the hand which held the plate.

Without any warning, Rikki launched himself at the offending hand drawing blood the colour of the strawberry tarts themselves. The plate fell and broke. The cream carpet stained immediately with strawberry gel, cream, tart and blood. A diabolical disaster. Apologies were not enough. Rikki was taken to the car immediately and told he was a very naughty dog. The atmosphere was strained for the rest of the afternoon as the women tried to eradicate the red and white matter from the pure white carpet.

When I heard the story I confirmed Rikki was not naughty at all. I coaxed him up to my bedroom and got him onto the bed beside me. I informed him he was a very good dog indeed and what he did must never be done again but he got the right victim and that made it a holiday to remember. Justice takes many forms and may be delayed for some time but only Rikki and I knew just how sweet revenge could possibly be.

Rikki settled after that into the family without any further problem. He enjoyed his clippings in summer as Poodles have to have their wool cut, as they have no casting hair. That also accounts for the numerous Poodle Parlours which through necessity also encourages the negative status of this fancy French breed. Why must they call it Poodle Parlour? Why not Pause to Trim or Tails to Tell. I am sure with a little greater thought a more imaginative name could be chosen for so many of these dog-clipping services.

We enjoyed Rikki's athleticism and vest for life, even his reputation at times for being Rikki the Rogue as he raced around the dining room table leading like Red Rum over the crouched children's backs, frustrating his progress. We had no inkling that this contentment was soon to end.

My mother after years of duty to a growing family and the family of the church too, decided to return to work. She became an occupational therapist at the Meanskirk Hospital set in the recuperative green hills of south Glasgow and Renfrewshire. She encouraged tapestry, helped patients write personal letters and supervised their creation of birthday and other celebratory cards. Visiting the open day-wards, set on the ground floor, came one of the nurse's dogs, Czar. Czar was the friendliest of black Labradors and popular too with the patients. Although I did not know it at the time, this would be the first of three black Labradors, I would enjoy meeting in later years.

One day a nurse was in floods of tears in the ward. Mother calmed her and enquired what the matter concerning her was. The cause of such misery was in fact a joyous occasion; or should have been. This attractive nurse had fallen in love with one of the doctors in the hospital. However the medical practitioner was a New Zealander and they agreed it was to the antipodes that they would go after they were married in the summer. Suddenly a gripping matter hit them hard. They could not take their beloved Czar and now needed to find a home for him as soon as possible. The thought of a dog pound from where its future would be uncertain brought tears to her pretty face. When mother heard this sad tale, and knowing the nature of this fine beast, there was an instant solution. Czar would come to the manse and join the family. We were thrilled to receive Czar. Such a dignified and regal name; such a stately dog.

Rikki was the only family member to have his nose put out of joint by this young new male arrival, as he, Rikki, was the senior dog, in the manse. No matter how patient Czar was, it was only when they were on leads for walks together did they acknowledge one another. Rikki barked at, bit and fought Czar on each and every occasion in the house. Two Alpha canine males were afoot. As a consequence they had to live in separate parts of the manse. How fortunate were the manse bairns to have such large manses to accommodate visitors and feuding dogs. This situation could not have been predicted and it must have made life difficult but I remember the need to close doors at all times. Dogs can be upset so easily. Some don't show their anxiety. Rikki wore his hurt in fighting Czar. It was not a pretty sight nor even a fair fight. Rikki never knew when he was beaten. And to be honest, I was away from home for much of their time together. Absence made the heart grow fonder of them but I did not experience the frequent separations. Like a boxing referee, Marjory separated the fighters who never heard the bell.

I had become engaged to be married to Jocelyn. A meeting of the families was expected of course but both Jocelyn and I were on contracts working in Ghana in West Africa where we met and could not return home. My parents decided to invite Dr and Mrs France to the manse at Glasgow for a weekend get-to-know each other. They arrived on Friday afternoon and introduced themselves. Mrs France had a liking for dogs, as she once bred Chows and so Czar was brought in to meet the guests but growling could be heard in the background. I think my parents-in-law would have been surprised that this canine aggression out of sight came from a woolly French Poodle.

Jocelyn and I from the heat of Africa hoped the meeting would progress amicably, in fact, it did with stories and tales being told on both sides of the family divide with neither of us being able to defend ourselves. There again our distance would hide our blushes too.

After the main course, Marjory returned to the kitchen and seemed to take ages before re-appearing. To keep the conversation going, Jim spoke.

'I hope you like lemon meringue pie with ice-cream.' His revelation was met with enthusiasm. Then Marjory arrived carrying a cut glass bowl of mixed fruit salad.

'Er......I was looking forward to .....the.... lemon meringue.....?' queried Jim.

Mum gave Dad a stern look as if to reprimand him but she realised the cat was out of the bag. (Ummm notice when a secret is out it's the cat we associate with this saying and never a dog.) Honesty as she always taught us, was the best policy.

'I have a confession to make. Czar managed to stand on his hind legs and without knocking the dish from the hatch, finished the lemon meringue pie. He had licked the plate so clean, I wondered if I had not removed the meringue pie from the oven!' she said.

It was said that this canine moment sealed the families together in friendship as they laughed heartily. Aye, we're a' Jock Tamson's bairns after all. Czar had his mischievous nature at times but Rikki was a rogue.

Chapter Notes

[1] Pet Ownership 2001 pp 815-820

Chapter 10
Black dog days

Sadly not all dogs take sanctuary in happy family homes, or simply enjoy the company of the human race. Kirrie and Rikki had their dark days but not as black as those dark black days of Diak and one unknown dog. I hope this paragraph prepares you for some grief. This is indeed a very sad chapter in my life of dogs.

I start with the story of Diak. He was the compound mongrel at the Presbyterian Church of Ghana at Tema where I worked in the 1970s. In the heat of the day, Diak was nowhere to be seen but as darkness fell each night at 6.30pm, every day of the year, he knew it was time to approach the open charcoal fire which would be cooking the communal meal. Pieces of fat or fish or chicken bone would be thrown in Diak's direction, landing on the reddish brown laterite ground. This dog was deprived of any human love and its nourishment was minimal. Its main duty was to keep the compound watchman awake if an intruder approached at an unearthly hour.

I took pity on Diak. I encouraged him to come to me at my home in the compound where I offered a few tasty scraps one day or a dried biscuit on another. Diak began to visit regularly and began to take food from my hand. But any attempt to stroke the dog's back or pat his head was quite out of the question. Snarling white teeth were quick to flash. But I did not give up easily. Speaking gently and feeding it regularly led to a degree of greater trust. But it took a considerable time. After all, I was the only white man this dog had encountered. If all the black people in his life kicked him or threw food at him, then it was surely a matter of time before I did the same he must have thought.

After the best part of a year, Diak and I had a better understanding. He would confidently come to my door, wagging his thin rope-like tail, fully anticipating some nourishment and he was rarely disappointed. But I noticed a lethargy creeping into him. When I drew close to him one night, I could see his stomach was full of lumps. His legs were bleeding slightly and his demeanour reflected his misery. When I mentioned his condition, the Ghanaian community took the view that it was only a dog. They would easily get another one. Veterinary services in Accra dealt with the tropical infestations of chicken, pigs, sheep, goats and wildlife. They had no small domestic pets section per se. Diak was condemned to a painful death.

The following day I kept Diak by my side by keeping a plate of meat out of reach. For the first time he let me feel his lumps. He knew he was ill. I could feel these bean shaped nodules moving around his body. With the gentlest of finger pressure on his skin, the culprits appeared. Maggots began to drop to the ground. I did not count them but I must have popped out some sixty of these agitated grubs. When I felt I had removed enough for one night, I could see the poor dog had streams of blood dripping from its sores. Aruna, the Mali Moslem night-watchman, prepared a bowl of warm water and I bathed Diak in a soapy bath. More maggots floated to the surface but Diak tolerated this treatment. Diak showed signs of gratitude for the first time in his life. I could pet him whenever I wanted now. Aruna gathered all the maggots from the front doorstep where I had been and set them on a metal tray in the forecourt.

'Food for de birds. Dey will chop dem all in di mornin.' And they did. So the food cycle was restored.

When I returned from four months sabbatical leave, there was no Diak in the compound. Naturally I asked about him. They told me he had died. I asked how he had died. I was informed that he went missing for a day, then they found him at the side of my house, dead.

There was no need for a post mortem, let alone further explanation. I have no idea how Diak died and I never found out. Animal deaths in much of the Third World do not generally cause much upset. They are not a priority. I understand without condoning their response.

One other dog whose name I did not even know met a very sad, yes even sadder end. I had taken the car, a bright new red Opel Ascona, a bucket-seated vehicle, which I received from the Church in Stuttgart, to the local Community One shopping centre in Tema. I parked near the Standard Bank of Ghana, a low square building with a significant veranda and four metallic boxes built into each side. These were not bank related as such. Their hum gave their purpose away. Banking was the coolest place to do business on the 0 degree longitude; 4 degree latitude location of Tema. There were few air-conditioned premises in Ghana in the early 70s.

It was a sizeable parking plot and when I put the hand brake on, I saw in the bougainvillea draped villa before me, a noisy disturbance taking place. The home owner saw me arrive and came running up to me. He was waving his hands and beckoning me to come to his house.

'Bring your car. You must run over the dog.'

'What? Why would I do that?' I asked.

'It has rabies. You must kill it. It is rabid.'

I had a dilemma. I saw the problem. The dog in question had been tied to the gate on a leash. It snarled at everyone approaching and saliva drooled from its open jaws. Then I saw the solution.

Behind me at the bank, sitting on his chair was a uniformed policeman with his rifle by his side. His colleague guarded the bank at the other side. These men were not part of the main police force. They were the auxiliary police force who wore the grey police shirts. They were illiterate, but loyal Ghanaian northerners, ideal to be guards and they took their duties seriously.

'Officer that man asked me to run over his rabid dog. It would not be easy to do and I don't think I could do that anyway. Can I ask you to come over and shoot the rabid dog?'

'No sah. I no come for to shoot de dog,' he said as he rose to stand at attention with his rifle by his side.

'But the other policeman can cover for you and the house is only a short distance away as you can see,' I pleaded.

The policeman was becoming more agitated.

'Then,' I said taking the bull by the horns, 'if you give me your rifle I will shoot the dog.' I was surprised at making this offer as I never thought I would ever fire a gun in anger. But hadn't I just asked an armed policeman to hand over his gun? On reflection, that sounded like a treasonable act on my part. My heart beat increased as I awaited his response.

'I can't, sah,' he said.

'Why ever not?' I asked.

He came towards me to whisper so no-one would hear.

'Please, what I go tell you, you must no go tell anyone.'

I had not expected this development. I gave him my word. (And now I break it.)

'You see, de Government, they no go trust us. Dey give us de gun but dey don't give us no ammunition for to put it in the gun. Now you no go tell anyone what I say, or de bank get robbed sum time.'

I agreed. I'd not of course divulge his occupational secret. But I now understood his anxiety. Just as I wondered what response was now needed, there was a sharp crack heard twice. I looked around at the house in question. The rabid dog lay on the ground dead by the gate entrance. It had been shot after all.

At home, dogs can get into serious difficulties too. The banks of the river Nith in summer are a pleasure to walk along. We can watch our dogs play near, or in, the gently flowing river, sometimes retrieving a ball or stick. (Better a ball, as sticks can lodge in a dog's throat). But in recent years, winter floods have become more common and the gently flowing river has become a grumbling caldron of aqueous danger.

Yet to the dog, it's still the place well known for a dip and a swim. The pull of water is strong and the dog enters the river. In time the river banks become like wet brown margarine. The dog fails to get any purchase as its claws sink into the mud. Unless a less angled gradient is nearby, the efforts are sapped away from the animal's survival instinct. The owner become distraught.

We tend to associate the Fire Brigade with ladders, flames and smoke. But today the Fire Brigade is a national service and its new name is The Scottish Fire and Rescue Service.

From time to time dogs require to be rescued. Of course cats climb onto telegraph poles and roofs and need to be rescued too but some water-loving dogs get into serious difficulty. When they do, its owner sometimes makes a fatal judgement to enter the water to rescue the dog. Others are clearer thinkers and dial 999 to alert the Scottish Fire & Rescue Service.

On 11 April 2012 a golden retriever entered the Nith. Retrievers and Spaniels, Poodles and of course the Newfoundland simply love the water and are strong swimmers. But this retriever was caught in the current like a wasp in a jelly jar. Energy had evaporated from its limbs. It was a matter of time before it would disappear under the fast moving water. It was a matter of canine life or death.

The picture I have included in this book is of the actual rescue of the Golden Retriever. You can see it was exhausted, but glad of being rescued from the river Nith, near Dumfries, after severe floods. What better way for me to acknowledge the work of the Fire and Rescue Service than by adding them to my list of supporters. Many dogs and other animals owe their lives to the Scottish Fire and Rescue Service. Their owners owe their profound gratitude.

Chapter 11
The Rev and the Thief.

By the time Jocelyn and I came home from Ghana, as a married couple, there was no Rikkie. His had been a full life ending in a battle of minds with Czar; an outmatched confrontation and one so completely unnecessary. Czar was the gentlest and accommodating of dogs.

One springtime we agreed to stay at the manse at Abernethy while Jim and Margery were at the General Assembly of the Church of Scotland at Edinburgh. Czar was walked in the morning, the afternoon and evening. It was a chore we happily did until one day, I came down with one of those bone weakening man-fevers. Jocelyn came up to the bedroom to see me.

'Czar. He's run away,' she said.

I felt the urge of responsibility and got dressed in a hurry.

'He's on the main road to Perth,' she said.

'What?'

So I ran and coughed, jogged and spluttered taking a breath every now and then to call his name. Thoughts of never seeing him again or that he was setting out to Edinburgh to find his real carers filled my mind. That seemed a real possibility. Dogs knew how to do just that.

Eventually I caught sight of him about two miles out of Abernethy. I called louder and louder. I saw him turn to face me momentarily then hesitantly, he continued for a few paces. He turned again as if to accept he had done wrong and began to walk towards me. As he approached, his tail was drooped down low. His expressive eyes told me he was sorry. I instantly forgave him. Labradors have that ability to make you feel weak at the knees. For me I was weak at the knees, the arms, the neck and the back. But Czar was with us again.

Never again did I hear of his wanderings. They never occurred. Perhaps he had been unsettled by our sudden occupancy of the manse.

During this time I was asked to speak about my work in Ghana in a church at Inverness and so to another manse we set out. The Reverend Fergus McNeil was the occupant, together with his Alsatian dog. It surprised me to learn that this dignified, strong yet soft dog answered to the name of Rev. As soon as we were introduced to each other, Rev was a real friend. His expressive eyes and his alert, erect ears made him seem a very intelligent dog and so he was.

We learned from Fergus that this softie had arrested a burglar one day when Fergus was out. He had returned to his manse and expected Rev to come bouncing to greet him at the front door but not this time. It put Fergus on edge. He mounted the staircase and saw Rev's tail in the first of four upstairs bedrooms. The Alsatian seemed to be stationary with its hairs standing up. Fergus knew something was definitely amiss as Rev had not responded to his approach on the creaking wooden staircase. When Fergus entered the bedroom, he noticed a man's legs under the bed and the bedroom window was open. Adrenaline coursed through his veins as Rev did not take his eyes off the burglar intruder.

Fergus gave out an order to Rev. One he had never heard before. 'Guard' he said. Rev lowered himself into a squat position. Presumably that loud instruction required some sort of response.

'Bite if he moves,' he said closing the bedroom door leaving the nervous pair alone in the room and flew down the stairs to telephone 999.

Minutes later the police arrived and with truncheons drawn they entered the bedroom.

'Sir, call the dog off I don't want to get bitten,' said the sergeant.

'Rev bite? I assure you officer, he's more likely to lick your face clean than bite it.'

The burglar was removed from under the bed and handcuffed. He did not speak but he gave Rev such a look as if to say, 'If I only knew you were toothless, I could have escaped.'

Chapter 12
Tâche is a stain

Jim and Marjory retired to Arbroath. When they arrived they were without a dog. Czar had passed on. But there was much to do in this seaside, fishing and historic town. It is known for its Smokies; the Arbroath Declaration of Independence; the coastal walks; Kerr's miniature train service by the seafront; an attractive harbour and not one but several choirs and dramatic productions of the highest calibre. It was, and is, a friendly town welcoming holiday makers from the central belt in summer and entertainment *par excellence* for the locals in winter.

Jim and Margery soon sampled all of these delightful offerings and became part of the community with Jim installed Chair of the Lifeboat Fund and a member of the male voice choir. Of course they had also signed up for dental, church and surgery membership.

Dr Meg Manson was their GP and she had a collie in season. In time, three collie pups arrived in her home with remarkably good markings and in fine health. She suggested to Jim that to keep up his exercise in retirement, he should have a dog. Jim thought that a possibility, with some reservations about his increasing age, but before he could change his mind, he had one of Dr Manson's collie puppies in their final home. The years rolled back to that first hesitant purchase of his first collie, Glen. It seemed that once an owner has had a particular breed before, pleasant memories come flooding back to influence the next doggy decision. That was Jim's experience.

It would not be fair to extend the similarities and name the dog Glen or Glen 2 of course. Each dog deserves its own nomenclature and thus its personality. Jim would have to think of another name for this handsome male dog.

The following morning while drinking his morning cup of Douwe Egberts coffee in his study, Jim noticed a slight imperfection on the dog's rump. It was as if the dog had brushed past a wet paint brush. No more than three hairs were white in a sea of a jet black back. Then a spark hit Jim. He called Margery.

'I've got the perfect name for him. You will never guess,' he teased.

Marjory always liked a challenge. 'Flash?....Luath or Ceasar ?' asked Marjory recalling the Twa Dogs of Robert Burns.

'No......I'll give you a clue.'

'No, not yet. Broath? ....Firth?...Crag?'

'No I've got to tell you, we'll call him, Tâche,'

'Tâche ? He hasn't got a moustache. People will think that's a daft name for a collie,' said Marjory.

'No it's not. Look here at his back. See these three white hairs? It's like a stain.....and that in French, that is *une tâche*,' said Jim triumphantly.

'Hmmm I see. Yes, I like it as a word. It's a good abrupt one syllable name. So Tâche it is then, Tâche?'

And Tâche looked up at his mistress. He already knew it was his name.

Jim had always loved the French language. He was a Francophile who was deprived his student year of study abroad in France as he, like Hitler, was planning to go to Paris, in September 1940.

Over time we had two young daughters Fiona and Laura. Fiona was the older of the two and had started to grow long legs. Tâche too was growing quickly and he too had long legs. He seemed to sense a similarity in Fiona who loved to chase him around the back garden and on the golden sands of Lunan Bay. It was a game he loved as his owners were now in their seventies and not nearly as nimble.

Our family enjoyed the Easter, summer and autumn breaks when we could come to visit. Tâche was always excited to see us. Walks in Glen Clova, Glen Prosen and around beautiful Lintrathen Loch were at the end of a fairly short drive and Tâche loved the car boot. He jumped into it as soon as the door was open. He dared not risk being left behind. Picnics of hot tea and biscuits accompanied these outings and a few dog biscuits were devoured too, by Tâche of course.

Then one Sunday as I was ironing in a state of oblivion, the telephone rang. Jocelyn answered the call. As I ironed, I saw on television, a discussion about the outrageous flighted kick administered into the crowd by Manchester United's mercurial star, Eric Cantona at Crystal Palace's Selhurst Park the previous afternoon. I was a little distracted when Jocelyn came though and placed her hands on my shoulders and gently caressed them.

'Miller that was your mother. Your father died this morning.'

The funeral took place the following week in Arbroath and Tâche knew what was happening. He was grief stricken too to have lost his night walker and the man who had taught him French instructions. His demeanour was depressed. He had lost his leader. He definitely sensed the finality of life.

As normality resumed in Arbroath, Mother put out a call to us in Dumfries.

'Would you take on Tâche? He's a family dog really and he knows you all so well.'

This seemed such an obvious decision and one which the girls looked forward to experiencing. Jocelyn was not going to stand in their way although she had in mind some house rules. So the following weekend we returned to Arbroath and on the Sunday afternoon we returned to Dumfries with Tâche in the car. The chatter of the girls and their music, played loudly on the car radio, made Tâche think he was about to experience a seismic change of lifestyle, and he was.

First the dog who had the freedom of the Arbroath home, found his basket in the kitchen and Jocelyn telling him that that was his bed. She did not want him upstairs in our bedroom and by his drooping head and his tail between his hind legs, he had understood her wishes.

On that very first night however, he crept up the stairs without us hearing him. He entered our bedroom and knowing that I had not given him the embargo, he came to my side of the bed and as was his want, collapsed his bones on the wooden floor. He had given the game away. But Jocelyn relented and in time, Tâche shared his rest each night starting off on my side of the bed and then around three o'clock, moving to go to Jocelyn's side of the bed. Tâche was always fair, sharing his love evenly.

The second significant alteration was in commands. I knew Jim had taught him French commands but how many and which ones, I did not recall. So a re-education took place. Tâche took that in his stride. He was always keen to learn. Not many dogs are bi-lingual.

It seemed that he liked a game of surprises too. Instead of handing him a biscuit reward, he was shown the biscuit and then the door was closed shutting him out. The girls then secreted the biscuits around the lounge. On the soft piano pedal, under the brass Buddha, under a poofee and one on the toe cap of my crossed legs, the doggie biscuits were placed.

Tâche entered with purpose, his tail wagging excitedly. First he saw the biscuit on my shoe. It was after all, at his eye level. But his mouth did not take it. He lifted his paw and knocked the biscuit from my shoe then ate it. Then behind the sofa he moved smartly to the Bechstein piano. The second treat was consumed. But the Buddha had sealed its vision and scent.

'One more Tâche. Seek, where is it?'

Tâche reached the coffee table. At first sight there was nothing on the glass top but somehow he had found the scent.

'Yes, Tâche, where is it?'

That was the encouragement he needed and the permission required and so he pawed at the Buddha who fell from grace to the carpet and the round biscuit came into view on the brass Buddha's wooden base.

Now that he had been given permission to knock the Buddha over, it became his favourite hunting place when the biscuits were hidden. It was a game of pitting our wits against his. Ever alert collies always enjoy a cerebral challenge.

Tâche had arrived in April and we had already booked a train journey to France that summer and that meant an arrangement had to be made for Tâche's care. After several conversations with dog owners we agree to have him booked into a rural Annandale kennel.

It is never easy to leave a dog in kennels but with the children excited about a south France coastal holiday, they soon realised that Tâche was at his holiday hotel where food, shelter and walks would keep him fed, sheltered and exercised amongs some new friends.

Of course the welcome we received when we returned is one reason why humans love their dogs. Completely forgiven, hardly containing his excitement, he wanted to greet each family member and get into the back of the car to go home as soon as possible.

In early December it was our youngest daughter's birthday. It was arranged that we would go as a family to Edinburgh some seventy five miles away, where a birthday present would be purchased for Laura. Somehow we had to make an arrangement for Tâche, as it was the first time he would be left in Dumfries all on his own.

We had secured the back garden on all four sides. He would have the run of that area. If it got cold or if he wished a drink, we would have that available in the conservatory where we had also placed his basket. The inner doors were snibbed shut to allow the security alarm to be activated. In the knowledge that it was 10 degrees Fahrenheit at the start of the month, we could not imagine he would catch a chill.

We arrived at Lockerbie station only to find the trains had been cancelled due to heavy snow on the line, miles south of the town. So we set out up the Beef Tub road to the capital.

As we climbed the Devil's Beef Tub north of Moffat the first snowflakes fell. We proceeded. The snow became much thicker and fell continuously. But as we reached the outskirts of Edinburgh, the city's warmth meant just wet streets. We spent around three hours in Auld Reekie then decided not to risk the snow on the rural back road, but cross over to the M74 motorway which was bound to have been kept clear. Nevertheless, at Harthill it became a whiteout. We stopped.

We telephoned our Dumfries neighbours who informed us that no snow was in the town but the police had just been to our house after a break-in. Be prepared for the worst he informed us.

We cautiously proceeded and eventually the snow cleared and our thoughts remained concentrated on the break-in. When we arrived home, Tâche was inside the house to greet us and a note had been left on the staircase by a Police Inspector. What transpired took some time to comprehend.

It appears that Tâche managed to work the conservatory door free and entered the house, thus setting off the burglar alarm. The Dumfries Police arrived promptly and gained access through the conservatory. At first Tâche had been on guard and the police approached cautiously. However Tâche let them continue with their investigation.

The note asked us to check older daughter Fiona's bedroom; the room at the top of the stairs. The room had been riffled but the other rooms seemed to be untouched. We were asked to report any losses in Fiona's room and of course anywhere else but somehow the Police thought the intruder had concentrated on Fiona's room. Perhaps he had been disturbed.

Well our daughters are like chalk and cheese. Laura keeps an immaculate bedroom while her sister Fiona has a more laissez-faire approach to her room and its possessions. Perhaps that is a little too generous a summary. Fiona's room sometimes seems to be a tip or a pigsty. That is why the Inspector felt there may have been a break-in. But it was a break-through for us and something we would never do again. From then on, Tâche was the back seat occupant.

I began working with Unex. This is a service that records the time a letter is in transit to its destination. It checks up on our Royal Mail service. If I were to tell you it is around 96% successful in the UK you might think there was room for improvement. I doubt if it could improve. As long as letters are sent without addresses and postcodes, they will get lost. Yet so many postmen are worth their weight in gold as they decipher handwriting, alter wrong postcodes and forward to new addresses as soon as they know there is a change. But I do not do this just for the UK. I do it for the entire world. Letters are sent to Chile and New Zealand one day, Romania and China the next. And I receive letters every day from every corner of the world. But it is the outgoing mail that involved Tâche.

I piled the letters by the front door each night and somewhere after 10pm, I would put on my coat and Tâche would be ready for his instruction.

'Post, Tâche.'

The door was opened and Tâche would set off at speed out of the drive, turning right, he would race along the pavement, out of sight as he turned the corner on the busy Edinburgh Road and sat motionless by the post-box. It would take a further four minutes for me to arrive and post the mail.

Then if the road was clear, I'd instruct him to cross. He never crossed the road without an instruction, even if the road was clear. I could then confidently take the decision not to have him on a lead, unless absolutely necessary.

The police began to notice Tâche's crouched position as he awaited to cross the busy main road to and from the town. One day a police car pulled up beside us and the police man left his car and approached with a smile.

'That dog of yours. I've seen it many times crouch in that position as if it's about to sprint across the road. He's doing a great service slowing drivers down,' he told me.

Chapter 13
They are not human, are they?

Dogs are not human. That is obvious. They do not have our intellect but they do of course, understand many commands. This was certainly true of Kirrie, Rikki and Czar. But both Glen and Tâche were in a different league. Was it because they were collies? Or did they possess an additional trait?

Perhaps it was by inclination and willingness to serve for years, or of successful breeding, but the working collie has many demands on it, in the fields. It is not a fireside-sleeping dog but one who lives outside happily; one ready to bark on the farm if disturbed by an oil thief or the too early arrival of the milkman. One who knows its duty to his master and the master knows what it can do, more than it cannot. And when its days are done working, the farmers do not carry an aging useless dog. New dogs have to be selected and trained and so, many farmers' aging collies are laid to rest, prematurely sometimes.

Tâche came from a long line of active sheepdogs. Sired by Jix at a farm near Thornhill (International Sheep Dog Society No: 154800) his mother was the Dam, Corrie (ISDS No: 170888) from J. W. Manson of Arbroath. Farmers knew how to improve a collie's breeding stock and it took time to find the right bitch. But that may be a universal search for all beings.

So Tâche had that favourable start to life but it still did not make him human. One weekend we visited Marjory and on the Saturday afternoon we arranged to go to Kirkcaldy in the Kingdom of Fife to see my uncle Stanley. Stanley was the fourth of five boys, Jim having been the eldest. To most people Stanley and Jim were easily distinguishable. Stanley had a more round face to Jim's more oval visage. Jim was a few inches taller and had a darker complexion. They walked in a different manner; Stanley with slightly more splayed feet and Jim with an almost military march. In fact they were two individuals who showed few signs of fraternal similarity, to the human eye.

When we arrived, Tâche jumped out of the car. When the front door opened, Tâche ran fast to meet and ecstatically greet Stanley as if this was Jim whom he had not seen since his death six months previously. This was the greeting Jim always received from Tâche and his brother, now taken aback, began to realise why Tâche was acting this way. Then Tâche withdrew slowly trying to understand why Stanley did not greet him as enthusiastically in the same way Jim had. It confused him and this was plain for all to see. He had quite mistaken the home owner. Perhaps if I only saw in black and white I might have had some difficulty sight wise, but to mistake Stanley for Jim was staggeringly remarkable. A definite failing? Or perhaps it was an insight of similar genes finding a common denominator, unknown to the human but recognised by the canine world?

It was winter. Scraping the ice off the car was a regular chore. My evening walks were taken with care but Tâche relished the freshness of the evening coldness. The coat that was excessive in summer was now a warm outdoor blanket.

I usually arose around 6:45am. As soon as I was up, Tâche was at the door. His early morning walk was to cross Dumfries & County Golf course then turn right along a pathway and return after we had reached the bank where we often disturbed ducks in winter, the kingfisher and heron in summer. It was a walk that took twenty-five minutes and when I returned Jocelyn would have been starting to eat her breakfast.

I donned suitable warm attire and opened the front door. Like a bullet Tâche set off up the drive and waited for me to open the gate to the golf course when I reached there, two minutes later. But Tâche waited in vain that morning.

I set off at a good speed but only took eight steps. As my heel came down on the patio bricks, black ice met my step and propelled me into the air. My hands went out to break the inevitable fall. When I descended, it was the back of my head which met the drive first. I was literally knocked out cold.

I have no idea how long I lay prone on the ice; my body heat eventually created a dry outline as I grew colder and colder.

My consciousness came back as my face was being licked and I heard a plaintive painful canine cry, not a bark but a concerned whine. Then a bark to alert Jocelyn. I became aware of my position, sat up and Tâche began to wag his tail. His walk was back on the cards.

It took a further moment to check no bones were broken. My hand produced no blood when I touched the cranial point of contact but a bump was there. I turned to look at the house then at Tâche up the drive awaiting my first step forward. My instinct was renewed. I followed him cautiously. His morning walk was sacrosanct.

Recalling our early meetings with Tâche, he was always ready to play with our two girls. He was un-used to spritely girls and would follow them wherever they went. When they went upstairs, he would follow.

One day when he was still in Arbroath, I followed Tâche upstairs with my camera. He had not had any close photographic encounters before and so he watched as I prepared to take his photograph. His interest was noted in his slightly leaning head and bright eyes. But with his paws folded on the top step, a regular habit of his, the photo did make him seem to be somewhat camp! I think you will recognise with ease that photograph.

In Dumfries a few years later he took up a similar pose. He found a comfortable position on the carpet at the top of the stairs. It became one of his favourite spots and it was not difficult to see why. That vantage point gave a clear view of human traffic from the kitchen to the front door; the lounge to the kitchen; from the kitchen to the dining room and from all three rooms to the toilet. That was how he knew exactly what everyone downstairs was doing. Anyone upstairs he did not mind as they would have to pass over him to descend.

But the second reason was very practical. The central heating pipes run underneath the ascending stairs to the radiator at the top landing. That meant a warm flow of water in winter would give him a most comfortable position as he studied the flow of people downstairs. But should the postman or any visitor ring the bell, he was down stairs in a flash, barking at the moving object in front of the frosted door window. Postmen soon knew it was not a threatening bark but an announcement to the family that there were letters to gather or a visitor to entertain. We rarely had to restrain him when the door was opened.

One Boxing Day when we were at the table with the curtains drawn, the door bell rang and as usual Tâche set off to inform us that we had a visitor.

Our visitor was a near neighbour who fish-farmed in the UK and in several other European countries. When the door was opened the eyes of a three foot salmon met Tâche's. There was hardly a fin's width between both sets of eyes. There was a brief standoff while Tâche assessed whether this was a live being or not. It sort of moved but that seemed to be due to the exchange of hands as the fish was presented as a Christmas gift. A further sniff of the glazed fish determined that Tâche would show no further interest until the fish was thoroughly cooked and in his dish. When it had been prepared, Tâche showed his appreciation of this fishy delicacy by leaving a very clean dish indeed.

This was unusual. Tâche received his daily meal at 6. 30 pm every night. When called, he would ignore us. On returning from his late evening walk, he often took a drink of water and began to eat his evening meal. But only a few mouthfuls were consumed. Yet in the morning when we came down to breakfast the bowl was not only finished, but licked-clean. Eating a little regularly throughout the day is thought to be healthy for human beings. It came naturally to Tâche.

But in 2002, to celebrate our silver wedding, my wife and I returned to Ghana as we had so many friends there. Our daughter who was a student at Glasgow University at the time wished to look after Tâche when we were away.

We took Tâche to Glasgow on a cold icy 2nd January 2002 and he knew immediately he was heading to Fiona's flat. After we had gone to the airport early the next morning, Fiona took Tâche out for his first Glasgow morning walk. However it was icy and Fiona fell on the pavement and bruised her knee. Tâche was quick to realise her problem and did not stray from her side on Gardner street. Perhaps he had learnt from my ice fall.

On our return from Ghana some three weeks later we learned that despite providing all his prepared meals, Tâche had been thrilled by the generosity of student life in Glasgow University's student union and had taken delight in polishing off the throw-away contents of chicken korma take-a-ways, fish and chips and chapattis. It was his winter holiday too and what pleasures he encountered in the student world.

It's easy to walk a dog in summer. There is a carefree spirit, unrestricted clothing and an ample amount of vitamin D free for the walker. Mid winter is different. Clothes are heavier and footwear takes longer to don. Further delays in the hall to locate scarves and gloves irked Tâche until the door opened. But he required and awaited an instruction. If I said 'car' he would wait until it reversed out of the garage. If I said 'post' he would sprint to the post box. If I said 'river' he would turn left at the top of the drive and race hell for leather to the golf course gate. There he would await its opening, in a few minutes time. During that time he would sit patiently for me.

After crossing the first hole, we would set across the practise holes to an open gate. (The public have a right of way across The Burns Walk on the County Golf course.) Options then are to turn left or right at that point and Tâche would await a further instruction. If it was an early morning walk it would be for the shorter walk to the right and Tâche knew that instinctively, but at the weekend, or any other time, his master might suddenly decide to walk along the bank the other way. That often meant a sharp turn and a turn of speed to take him ahead of his walker.

It was on the shorter walk one chilly day, after the course deployed the winter tees, that Tâche sat and stared at the temporary winter tee of hole number 5. His gaze drew my attention. There, I read the name of the hole, Spion Kop. The name rang a bell in my memory. I recalled the name as being the Spion Kop an infamous battle in the Boer War at the turn of the last century.

When I returned home I consulted a rather old colonial book entitled: With the Flag to Pretoria. Tâche had brought my attention to the Battle of Spion Kop on January 17-22nd 1900. Winston Churchill after his capture and escape as a journalist in South Africa was appointed by General Butler as a Lieutenant in the South African Light Horse. In that role he reported on the progress of the battle for the hill.

'Bodies lay here and there. Many of the wounds were of a horrible nature. The splinters and fragments of the shells had torn and mutilated them. The shallow trenches were choked with the dead and wounded.'

Interestingly, Mohandas Ghandi served here in the uniform of a warrant officer of the Indian Ambulance Corps.

The Cameronians, a Scottish battalion recruiting from the south of Scotland, arrived to assist the taking of the Kop but that night Colonel Malby Crofton of the Royal Lancastrians lost his nerve and inexplicably by morning, the British had retreated, leaving the Kop to the Boers.

So why was hole number 5 named Spion Kop? Investigations discovered the Dumfries County course was designed and opened in 1904. At that point the eighteen holes would have been named, two years after cessation of South African hostitilies. When they observed the terrain of this hole, they could see the similarity of the Spion Kop's gradual incline and then a steeper climb to the top. This Dumfries Golf Club hole starts off on the flat but soon begins to rise. The green is actually out of sight on top of the hill. Surely a surviving and returning Cameronian would have recognised the salient? And that is why Dumfries Golf Club named hole number 5 as Spion Kop and why Liverpool Football club named their home tiered stand as the KOP in memory of the Royal Lancashire Regiment who along with their comrade Cameronians fell at Spion Kop in the Boer war.

The press took interest in this story as the centenary of the battle approached and so Tâche and I were called to the tee in question and had our photograph taken to accompany the press narrative.

Tâche excelled in another remarkable feat. He rarely barked but he did give a remarkably loud wolf cry. It was not a nocturnal sound as you might imagine under a new moon but it was almost daily. The strident chords of the daily News, or at the weekend, Match of the Day gave him his opportunity. Monday night brought Panorama and on Thursday Question Time. Each opening theme tune irked him as soon as he heard these strident theme tunes, he howled. Awooooooooooooooo. It did not take me long to recognise that I watched the daily news bulletins religiously; Question Time's Thursday evening spot was sacrosanct as was Saturday evening's Match of the Day. Was Tâche making me aware the programme was about to start? I think that might have been the case.

There were of course two other members of the family growing up and for Fiona and Laura, the Australian soap series, Neighbours, was a regular teatime viewing necessity. And to make sure they never missed the start of the programme, Tâche let out one of his amazing howls. Was he doing this service for them or was this another opening musical theme which terrified Tâche and he let us know? He did not respond like this to all programmes. Far from it. When Eastenders began, for example, with its emblematic theme tune, Tâche ignored it. But Casualty was another programme he'd summons Granny to see with his call when she came to stay with us and at her home in Wigan. So my careful study of his wolf cry outbursts showed that Tâche had associated different people with their favourite programmes and chosen to announce to them that their programme was starting. Either that or he found the BBC themes a pain in his ears.

Not long after Tâche came to live with us Fiona our eldest daughter took ill. Her recovery was not instant but when we saw signs of recuperation we decided to spend a weekend at the Stranraer's North West Castle hotel. One of the main reasons we chose this hotel was that its owners, the McMillans, did not deter well behaved dogs as guests. As long as they stayed in their owners rooms, all would be well. Dogs were certainly not allowed into the dining room under any circumstances. That could lead to unfortunate canine quarrels and potential mayhem.

Tâche was not sure of his room. At night he prowled around before settling by my side of the bed. In the daytime, there were seaside and coastal walks and walks in the Galloway hills but at night he was left in the bedroom while the family dined on Galloway scallops; roast deer and to finish, the wonderful amusingly named local dish, the Ecclefechan Tart. After the delights of the tart, I ordered a coffee while Jocelyn left the table to give Tâche a final evening walk.

Tâche always walked by his master or mistress's side in unfamiliar territory. He set off with Joce along the corridor and down the stairs. Then Tâche appeared at the doorway of the hotel restaurant and raised his nose. It may have been to appreciate the delights of braised steak or perhaps the delicate fragrance of fennelled halibut. However his nostrils also gave him the information he required and he came to our table and settled down underneath, content to recognise the family's legs.

Familiar with the etiquette required, I tried to coax Tâche out from his haven and return him to Jocelyn to continue his nocturnal walk. But the staff saw he was a contented dog lying under the table, causing no disturbance and so Tâche was allowed to remain until we left the table to the dying chords of Moon River played by the hotel's pianist.

Tâche loved the car. Whether it was a long trip to visit either grandparent at Wigan or Arbroath made no difference. He could sleep as long as the wheels were turning. But on a Sunday afternoon, in the car, it meant a walk. He became very excited. He knew when we accelerated out of Dumfries that we would be heading for Mabie Forest. The remainder of the journey was accompanied by a strained cry and the occasional muffled bark. He was excited.

On summer holidays he came with us to Devon. The back of the car was his. A full roof box enabled his comfort and when the boot door was eventually opened, he cowered his head and awaited the door to lift high above him before jumping out. Cautious was Tâche at times yet he also had a great turn of pace, especially when seeing a letter await the post box.

Walking handsome Tâche ensured I got to know many new neighbours who walked their dogs. Dog walkers want to know which dogs might cause problems and which may be too frisky. But equally they want to meet fellow friendly dog walkers and dogs. This process also helps us to overcome and talk about the loss of a dog as we are quick to notice an absent walker or a walker with a new charge.

Tâche was slowing down. That we could accept and accordingly did not place any demands on him. But the signs were there. One day I took him for a walk and as usual he never wore a lead. Always he awaited my command to cross the road and Edinburgh road is a very busy road indeed, at all times of the day. He sat by my side as the cars passed. I did not move or make any sound but Tâche decided to cross. He had never done this before. I looked up and saw a large lorry bear down from the roundabout and cars from the other direction approach. I screamed at Tâche to come back but he froze. His vision was not clear. I ran into the road and grabbed his collar and returned him safely to the pavement. Tâche seemed to know there had been danger.

It was his eyesight which failed first. Then the water retention problems arose. No longer was he interested in going outside. I slept on the lounge floor with him but I knew this was no longer that vital member of the family. His eyes expressed it so clearly; his time was up.

We telephoned the Bard's Vets and Alan Marshall who had seen Tâche at his regular appointments over the years came out the next day, a Saturday. Tâche lay on the lounge floor and did not move. I lay down beside him, caressing his folded ears. Alan shaved his paw and Tâche did not mind. He seemed to sense this was the seminal moment.

I held Tâche's head as the needle entered a vein. His head lost its neck muscles and fell back into my hands. I laid him down. Not a twitch or a frown. A perfect end. Alan produced a strong black bag. I took it from him and we helped Tâche enter out of sight. I offered to take the bag to Alan's car and did so, leaving Tâche on the back seat of his car. I patted his body. It was firm but lifeless.

Chapter 14
The Police came calling.

After Tâche died in November 2005 I was appointed the camp manager of Mundihar in the NWFP of the Islamic Republic of Pakistan after the devastating earthquake of October 2005. Since Allah loves every creature, He has made the principles of mercy and compassion to be extended to every living creature.

'All creatures are Allah's children and those dearest to Allah are those who treat His children kindly' (Baihaqi).

In a country which insists in the visitor and family members removing their outdoor shoes before entering a house, it was not surprising that the dogs I saw in Pakistan were usually guard dogs living out of doors. During my three months in the North West Frontier Province, I never got to know any dog and saw very few indeed. In fact as Malala Yousafzai says in her autobiography, I am Malala, referring to General Musharraf, as "a man who occasionally dressed in Western suits and called himself chief executive instead of chief martial law administrator, he also kept dogs, which we Muslims regard as unclean."

Dogs constantly keep themselves clean and are rarely known to spread disease to humans. If they did, we too would regard them as unclean and not have them in our homes.

On my return home from Pakistan, I received a telephone call. It was from a lecturer at the Bell College of Nursing (now the University of South West Scotland). She realised

I had written a book about Memory Loss (qv Have You Seen My.....Ummm...Memory?) She invited me to give a weekly one hour lecture on memory loss to her final year nursing students. I agreed. That was where I learned the self evident truths that canine friends make people less lonely, a Best Friend staves off negative feelings and this is backed by research.[1] However it should be noted that pets of all descriptions are an extra facet of social support and not a replacement.

I also learned that the lecturer, Anna Waugh, had two Schnauzer dogs. I offered to look after them while she was working but Anna had made alternative arrangements for her dignified, bushy eye-browed Schnauzers. Instead she arranged for her sister-in-law to see me about walking their dog, a black Labrador.

Constable Jane Dunbar arrived one day with Bobby. In tow were Shannon and her brother Ronan who soon made their way to the back garden to play with Bobby. I agreed to walk this beautiful and fit young black Labrador Bobby, every possible weekday morning and as a result was given a front door key to the Dunbar household.

That Monday morning I arrived at their door. The only occupant was Bobby. His mistress was at work as was his master as Manager at the Your Move estate agents. The children were at school and hence my *raison d'être*, as the dog walker. I entered the house and as I stepped forward into the hall, I was confronted by a large black Labrador who certainly was not expecting an intruder. He growled a low menacing noise. My encouraging words calling his name made little difference. Still the low growl was warning me and the sharp hazel eyes penetrated my glances. I had not expected this reception. But it is reassuring for all dog owners whose pet faces an unknown visitor on its own, that its instinct is to protect his home.

I decided to open the French doors and enter the back garden. Bobby followed and then I asked him if he wished a walk. The words were familiar to him and so I re-entered the kitchen, closed fast the patio French doors and found his lead. Now that it was in my hand, I had gained his interest and he came bounding towards me happily. No sooner was the outside door closed than we were off on our first of many walks in all weathers and all directions

Since then, we have had eight years of week-day walks on the banks of the Nith, at Mabie forest, the Heathhall cycle path and sometimes to town. Over these years Bobby has shown an interest in meeting many other dogs just as I have in the dog walking fraternity of Dumfries but I do have to admit regularly and reluctantly that Bobby is not really my dog.

One game Bobby enjoyed was to have a stick thrown down a steep embankment on the banks of the river Nith. He set off to retrieve it and when his breath was back, he was ready for another throw. It was during these games that I recognised the strong retriever element in this intelligent black Labrador. So began a game to collect fallen branches and deliver them to the gate to the golf course. Some of these sticks are really long logs; such are their weight and size but all have been collected by Bobby. (See photos to see the size of Bobby's log collection.) When the sticks have reached an appropriate height, the Community Pay Back scheme gather them, dry them, and then cut them into fireside logs for the elderly and infirm in our many rural communities.

But Bobby has other talents. Once on the narrow pathway along the river we approached three youths who were the worse of drink.

'Hey mister, is yer dog friendly?'

'He can be,' I said raising doubts in their minds, and more worrying thoughts in mine. Then telling a rather large white lie to extricate myself from what seemed to be a developing confrontation, I continued.

'He's a Police Dog. He sniffs for drugs.'

On hearing this statement the three boys threw away their special brew cans into the Nith and ran helter skelter from whence they had come. I sighed a big relief, feeling guilty that I had to rely on a lie. Well, a wee white lie, perhaps. After all Jane was a police officer and it was her dog. So it was a sort of Police dog. And I dare say with the keen sense of smell, Bobby could no doubt detect any illicit drug if he had been asked to do so.

Bobby has pleased so many golfers over the years. Not only by his good looks but he was quick to spot a golf ball veer off the fairway over the path and down the leafy embankment. On the command to seek, Bobby would set off and retrieve the golf ball much to the golfer's amazement. On one occasion he had just done that and waited the re-uniting of golfer with his ball when he decided to drop it. Unfortunately the ball landed on my toe and the ball returned down the embankment and plopped back into the river Nith. But Bobby had done his part and would not retrieve it again. After all it was me who sent it without reason, to its watery grave.

It's also a game at the start of the walk when we discover a golfer in the rough at the very first hole. On command once more to seek, Bobby's nose is grounded for the scent of the hand which placed the ball on the tee. On some searches, neither of us find the ball but on numerous occasions when the ball is found, the golfer smiles from ear to ear and expresses delight and amazement in equal measure. Bobby disregards the praise. After all, he is a retriever, it is natural to him. Some golfers wish Bobby to go round all eighteen holes to ensure they do not lose any more golf balls. But golf is not what some wish us to believe, a simple walk. Its hesitant progress would frustrate Bobby and certainly Blu if not every dog.

Bobby's cousin Buck is an almost identical black Labrador. He comes over to stay with Bobby when his owners are away. I then walk both dogs. As I walk on the main road with two black Labradors on one lead, with two connections to their collars, I feel like the landed gentry. To the eye, they do look very similar but their temperaments are slightly different.

Bobby always expects his rewarded biscuits after his walk will be thrown to him. He leaps to catch them. If I offered Bobby a biscuit directly to his mouth, his enthusiasm might lead to an innocent bite. But with Buck it is different. He expects to be handed a biscuit and he gently offers his open mouth for the biscuit to be placed on his tongue. I often wondered why such a difference occurred in related dogs. My conclusion might seem a little harsh but I suspect living with a young family makes Bobby very active; slightly more active than Frank and Christina perhaps and so Buck mirrors their less frantic lifestyle.

It was around that time in midsummer in an exceptionally warm period, when lethargy was seen in dogs as well as humans, we were asked to care for Hilda, my brother's dog, for ten days. The name Hilda is a feminine German name. It conjures up to mind a strident confident German woman. A sort of canine Frau Angela Merkel perhaps. There was nothing feminine about Hilda but if by Germanic you mean opinionated, then she certainly was. Hilda was a Basset Hound.

Instant friendship it provided and it was keen to share the couch with whoever seemed to sit the longest. One post lunch slumber in the soporific warmth of the conservatory floor I snoozed with Any Questions broadcast in the background. Hilda lay down beside me and stretched out. What a length. That long back and elongated legs fore and aft lay beside me from my chin to my shin. Hilda's broad protruding chest gave it an extra hand in deciding the softness or hardness of a surface but one specific surface intrigued Hilda. It was our dining table. Specifically it was one evening meal. Not his of course, but ours. Hilda would willingly eat anything which we regarded as food. Curry, figs, soup, stewed apple; the list goes on and Hilda expressed an interest in its production as well as its appearance.

One day I had hardly turned my back to announce lunch was ready to find a lettuce leaf being removed from a salad plate. And so the puzzling mix of the Basset hound personality became known to us; calm, most certainly; self-willed most definitely; most affectionate, beyond doubt and very stubborn and disobedient, yes in a sort of loving way. But he did excel in showing one proven ability. That is for a dog to yawn when empathising with its carer. There should be nothing to prevent me thinking therefore, that if I yawn in front of a dog, it will realise that I am empathising with it!

Each July when its owners are away on holiday in Florida, I take Blu for a walk. Blu is a Springer spaniel. Springer indeed. Blu becomes so excited when I arrive to walk him that he jumps up and nips me. In summer when I wear only a tee-shirt it has caused a painful nipple bite and at other times he seems to catch me in the stomach or the legs. He does not mean to injure me of course but no harsh word or delayed lead-collaring makes him desist. It's the welcome he gives unreservedly, typical of a Springer spaniel. However a sharp 'Heel' or 'Sit' is now proving successful as he awaits his lead.

In fact the way to deal with most jumping-up dogs is very simple. It requires the human to close his or her eyes. With no eye contact the jumping dog stops. Do try it for yourself. Unfortunately I learned this advice too late.

However once out of the gate, Blu is the perfect dog. As we cross the busy Edinburgh Road, I must restrain an eager Blu. If he was not on the lead, he'd run over the road and be run over. That leads to the public crossing to the golf course. At that point with ears trailing along behind an anxious head, Blu sets off at pace. A spaniel is not a retriever of course but it does appreciate a stick being thrown into the Nith. Blu dives over the leafy precipice and jumps into the water in all seasons. He's a great swimmer. Even a stone receives the same interest and it is of course a far safer projectile.

As soon as he's out he's ready again to dive into the bed of dried leaves on the embankment and then leap into the water again. But when he secures the thrown stick, he does not return it to me. He lands on terra firma and drops it on his way back to me. This way it's always a new stick or stone that must be thrown and thrown immediately. He burns up lots of energy. It certainly exercises him and keeps me on my toes.

Bobby does not miss out on a July walk as his is a mid-morning walk while Blu, mid-afternoon. I never walk both dogs together despite them living only three houses apart. That might be too difficult an undertaking and I'd prefer to concentrate and enjoy the behaviour and antics of each dog at different times.

Nearby there is one man who walks twelve dogs, all at the same time. It's a most strange sight. He has Jack Russells, Alsatians, Rottweilers, a Poodle and several Heinz 47s. For some, it must seem that they are a walking feast for the larger dogs! Somehow he manages to control them on one or two leads but I can't see how this strange sight, which I see on the Heathhall cycle path regularly, can attend to the necessities of dog walking. I think he needs to be re-educated.

One other rather special dog spends a day with me from time to time. He's a glowing white retriever named Ziggy. Without a look back at his departing owners, he settles at our home after he has been dropped off and swings into the Caldwell routine.

He bounds over the golf course and trots majestically on the path by the river. On my watch he has not gone swimming but I am sure in summer with gentle coaxing he might. When we return, I sometimes take a steel comb to his coat. He loves that. The resultant bundles of blond hair are gone by the morning, taken up by the birds which frequent our back garden. Some chicks are born in luxuriously lined nests, the product of Ziggy.

Ziggy like Tâche had a problem with entering the car boot. When young, Tâche would have no difficulty leaping in to make sure he did not miss out on a ride but in his latter years his spring had gone from his hind quarters and he had to be handled into the boot. So we bought a ramp. The ramp unfolded and was positioned at an angle from the ground to the car. The procedure seemed simple. But try as we might, Tâche never took to the ramp and so we gave it away to Ziggy who likewise found it beneath his dignity and did not use it.

Ziggy is by far the most regal of dogs. His aloof pose is striking but his sense of fun and activity is unquenching. He's a favourite with his grandchildren. Indeed a favourite with all he meets.

In October 2013 Bobby acquired a toy. It was a sort of anthropomorphic sexless toy, named simply 'baby'. Each day when I arrived to walk him, he greeted me at the front door then moved swiftly to the kitchen and lifted 'baby'. He then presented it to me. Meanwhile I continued to search for his collar or lead or both depending where it or they had been left. Sometimes in Shannon's room, sometimes in Ronan's. Sometimes just under his blanket. This was my preparation to get Bobby ready for his walk. But still 'baby' remained in Bobby's mouth. My instinct to remove it, I now realise was wrong.

When Bobby was ready to set off I'd ask him to 'Drop Baby.' Bobby did so somewhat reluctantly. This over his last few months became a ritual; his seizing of the toy baby and then the instruction to drop the baby.

What I now realise is that Bobby was presenting the catch to me. He was showing how capable he was as a Labrador retriever. I should have accepted his presentation and thanked him and not told him to drop it. Sorry Bobby for not understanding your gift. We can all fall out with family members and friends and we do so from time to time. But Bobby like so many other dogs was instantly ready to forgive. There is a lesson there for us humans too.

That year Bobby went with his family to Aviemore at Christmas and when he returned, I learned that he had had a seizure, rather like myself a year ago. Further tests revealed rheumatism of his hind legs, not uncommon for the Labrador breed, but sadly cancer in his kidneys too.

From being such an active, log-gathering, swimming and walking companion, his demise was sudden and painful to observe. One hundred yard walks for a dog that was used to speeding across the golf course to the river Nith was not the vital life I was used to seeing and neither was it familiar for Bobby. There was an understanding that did not much depend on any conventional means of communication between man and dog. In my relationship with Bobby I sensed, not mawkish sentiment, but something beyond scientific recognition, almost lost, but natural and ancient beyond the numbering of years.

Every dog will have its day and Bobby and I had our last valedictory walk at a steady, slow pace two days before he left us.

Note

A week after Bobby's death I visited his home and gave his family a copy of a video I had taken of Bobby in happier and sunnier times. He was actively retrieving a stick of course. This simple video last around 20 seconds. I mention this as it is something all dog owners should do. It is not a task to keep putting off, rather like making a Will. But your video will bring memories of an active happy dog just as you would wish your dog to be remembered.

And Bobby is remembered in Castle Douglas where he is buried in the rear garden of his owners' parents. A carved stone marks the spot and focuses the gratitude we had for this wonderful dog.

Chapter Notes

[1] Banks MR and WA 'The Effects of Animal assisted Therapy in loneliness in an elderly population in a long term facility. Journal of Gerontology Series 2002 M 428-32.

PART 3
REFLECTIONS

Chapter 15
Dogs reporting for duty

Man has throughout the ages defined the role of his dog in his life. The sheep-herding breeds are the best known in this capacity while the town dweller may be as familiar with the guide dogs for the blind walking along the streets. Labradors are particularly suited to that role. Poodles and Spaniels can be the ears of the deaf and of course the Alsatian is well known as a Police Dog and an RAF station guard dog and mascot.

The dog has been bred and fine-tuned over many centuries to the point that it serves his or her master well. The Hounds pursue game and if necessary prevent its escape. Hounds hunt with their noses to the ground in order to follow a scent or trail and they bark to inform and reassure master where they are engaged.

Hunting on horseback with a pack of hounds, a Boxing Day spectical, was popular with kings and noblement in France before coming to England. If the chase is live there will be opposition to a fine tradition. However the nation is divided. Can fox hunting be justified in this 'rights' age?

The greyhound hunts in a different way. Using its speed in Afghanistan it would outrun the game and with a short swift movements bring down the kill. But the track in Europe is where we associate its speed. Retired greyhounds surprisingly do not need much exercise. They are also the gentlest of dogs and very affectionate.

But that hunting instincet dominates in the hound breed whether it is a Bloodhound, Basset or Beagle.

woof

The word Terrier comes from the latin, terra, the word for earth. Hunting badgers and foxes by working their front paws into holes and digging is their expertise.

It is not surprising therefore that the ubiquitous Terrier is a temperamental and lively dog who is in its element with young people and a noisy family. Make no mistake none of the smaller terrier breeds are lap dogs. The Border terrier is seen often in the UK but more often locally in its southern upland homeland around Dumfriesshire and Cumbria.

woof

Utility or Guard dogs have a self evident purpose in life. There is a hereditary aptitude to guard and defend by these dogs, the Mastiffs being amongst the oldest of this category. It goes without saying such a dog is not best suited to appartment living conditions and postmen do not see such dogs as their favourite breed. But this group have always lived close to civilization and with fewer threats in a settled community, these dogs have adapted to being calm family pets. Within the family it would not be unusual for a sleeping child on the floor to have the close protection of the family Mastiff. Not so long ago in the tents of the nomadic tribes, children would curl up against the Mastiff or Spitz to keep warm at night.

woof

The Sheep-herding dogs have served farmers over thousands of years. They can be subdivided into mountain dogs (the oldest of this group) and shepherd or sheepdogs. Such dogs must have the instinct to control a large group of sheep or cattle, keep them together, be able quickly to understand the directions of the shepherd by call or whistle and be intelligent enough to take the initiative on their own. They have also been used as police dogs, guide dogs and for finding lost poeple in the snow. In recent years they have traced those in possession of illicit drugs and they can trace gas leaks too. They must be trustworthy. They are definately not suited to the nervous dog owner. Few humans have the staying power and the constant willingness to learn as the Border Collie.

woof

Two other categories of dog remain and I need not dwell on their innate abilities. They are the large companion dogs and the small companion dogs. The common link of companion gives the game away. These dogs are lively happy dogs following the mistress around the house, exuberantly greeting master and children of the family as well as their freinds and visitors. The Pug, French Bulldog and Boston Terrier will be happy in a quiet household and will be good company for the elderly. The Poodle and the Dalmation will be ideal playful companions for the teenager.

The smaller companion dogs such as the Yorkshire Terrier, the Pekinese and King Charles Spaniel can not be relied to perform beyond giving a few tricks but for exclusive friendship and companionship, these lap-dogs are in a league of their own. Although owners of other breeds may well disagree to some extent.

In brief, it is these differing considerations which lead us to decide on which dog to bring in to our homes. But we are now discovering further canine facts and abilities which will have a considerable impact on our future lives, the lives of our two footed friends and our communities.

woof

Many community groups invite Police dog handlers to their meetings. Often a spaniel attends and is asked to seek a previously hidden stache of illicit drugs. The dog proceeds through the seated members and around the room, lifting its head to sniff wall hangings from a distance until the drugs are found. Then the reward. No, not a handful of dog biscuits but a rubber ball is thrown and its bounce terminates in the jaws of the dog. It's a thrilling game for the spaniel and a wonderful service to the community.

Dogs are now working in the medical field too. Cancer has a nasty smell which we don't detect. But for Ulric, Ozzy and some other enthusiastic dogs at the Medical Detection Dogs HQ near Milton Keynes, it is a fantastic game. They have a regular 9am – 3pm working day in a Bio-Detection airy room where they play in 20 minute shifts, sniffing out cancer from different samples of urine.

It's a rather uninteresting liquid which dog walkers are relieved, I mean grateful, that they do not also have to clear from the pavement. But urologists can tell a lot from pee; how much you have drunk, if you have a kidney infection, or cancer and evidence of bladder, prostate and renal tumours which leave traces in urine. The human nose can not detect any of this. One dog Daisey, has flagged up 628 cases of cancer out of 6,100 samples.

A Mr. John Church a retired orthopaedic surgeon and maggot expert who used maggots to heal wounds, read a letter in the Lancet, in 1989. He read of a lady who was pestered by her pet dog paying much attention to a mole on her leg. Eventually the lady made an appointment with a dermatologist who promptly diagnosed early malignant melanoma. The story got him thinking. A few years later he heard a similar story. In Wellington College, Berkshire after giving one of his maggot lectures a student told him that his labrador had started to behave in a funny way trying to get to a patch of eczema on the back of his left thigh. The doctor treated the 'eczema' and a biopsy revealed early skin cancer.

It was while listening to the Today programme on Radio 4 in the year 2000 that Mr. Church responded to the programme's request by Dr. Clare Guest to find someone who would like to train a dog to detect cancer to get in touch with the programme. Guest and Church discovered they lived less than 20 minutes away and so a team began to work on the project.

What we do know is that a dog's hearing is more sensitive than ours; it can see more than us at night (and slightly less than us in daylight) but the brilliance of a dog, is in its nose.

woof

There is also a contagious cancer in dogs which has the ability to repair itself by acquiring mitochondria from its canine host's cells. The discovery could help to explain how this cancer, CTVT (Canine Transmissible Venereal Tumour), has remained in the dog population for around 10,000 years. It's hoped that future research may lead to preventions or cures for other transmissible cancers. Mating in dogs typically transmits the cancer, although it can also be spread when a healthy dog licks, bites or sniffs tumour-affected areas of a victim.

It has been argued by Professor Austin Burt, an evolutionary geneticist at Imperial College London, that when dogs were first domesticated, they were highly inbred and so different individuals were genetically very similar, and this might have helped cancerous cells from one dog to be able to be grown in another. Then, as dogs were bred in many different directions and became genetically diverse, the cancer would have evolved to be able to grow on a diverse array of genotypes.

The professor along with colleagues Clare Rebecca and Armand Leroi analyzed the cellular structure of a geographically diverse sample of CTVT samples. They noticed that the cancer would sometimes acquire the "powerhouses," or mitochondria, of host cells in order to repair itself in response to accumulated genetic mutations.

To determine if this was really the case, the scientists studied the evolutionary development of dogs and wolves. That investigation further supported their determination about the host-hijacking cancer. The research has been published. The disease is known to only spread from one canine to another, and "feral dogs -- ones that run wild are the ones most likely to come into contact with the cancer and carry it," according to Burt.

It is unclear, at present, if the new findings about cancer's ability to repair itself could apply to human cancer and to contagious cancers throughout the animal kingdom. However the breakthrough in knowledge of the canine investigation gives hope to humans and gives us another reason to be thankful to dogs. The good news about CTVT is that it can often be successfully treated on dogs with drugs. Professor Burt added, "many times the cancer is eventually recognized by the dog immune system and the dog recovers without treatment."

Dogs are become increasingly trained to detect human cancer growths, often unknown to the sufferer. Dogs can now even detect if someone has cancer just by sniffing the person's breath, a new study shows.

Ordinary household dogs with only a few weeks of basic "puppy training" learned to accurately distinguish between breath samples of lung- and breast-cancer patients and healthy subjects.

"Our study provides compelling evidence that cancers hidden beneath the skin can be detected simply by dogs examining the odours of a person's breath," said Michael McCulloch, who led the research.

Early detection of cancers greatly improves a patient's survival chances, and researchers hope that man's best friend, the dog, can become an important tool in early screening.

Biochemical Markers

That dogs aid a faster recovery to ailments is a self evident truth but they do much more than that. Dogs can identify chemical traces of cancer in the range of parts per trillion. Previous studies have confirmed the ability of trained dogs to detect skin-cancer melanomas by sniffing skin lesions. Researchers have established that dogs can detect prostate cancer by smelling patients' urine, as I said earlier.

"Canine scent detection of cancer was something that was anecdotally discussed for decades, but we felt it was appropriate to design a rigorous study that seriously investigated this topic to better evaluate its effectiveness," said Nicholas Broffman, executive director of the Pine Street Foundation.

Lung-and breast-cancer patients are known to exhale patterns of biochemical markers in their breath. "Cancer cells emit different metabolic waste products than normal cells," Broffman said. "The differences between these metabolic products are so great that they can be detected by a dog's keen sense of smell, even in the early stages of disease."

The researchers used a food reward-based method to train five ordinary household dogs. Encountering breath samples captured in tubes, the dogs gave a positive identification of a cancer patient by sitting or lying down in front of a test station.

By scent alone, the canines identified 55 lung and 31 breast cancer patients from those of 83 healthy humans. The results of the study showed that the dogs could detect breast cancer and lung cancer between 88 and 97 percent of the time.

The high degree of accuracy persisted even after results were adjusted to take into account whether the lung cancer patients were currently smokers. "It did not seem to matter which dog it was or which stage cancer it was, in terms of our results," Broffman said.

Different Wiring

According to James Walker, director of the Sensory Research Institute at Florida State University in Tallahassee, canines' sense of smell is generally 10,000 to 100,000 times superior to that of humans. It is unclear what exactly makes dogs such good smellers, though much more of the dog brain is devoted to smell than it is in humans. Canines also have a greater convergence of neurons from the nose to the brain than humans do.

"The dog's brain and nose hardware is currently the most sophisticated odour detection device on the planet," McCulloch, the study leader, said. "Technology now has to rise to meet that challenge."

Researchers envision that dogs could be used in doctors' surgeries for preliminary cancer detection. "There are lots of experimental treatments," Walker said. "This could be an experimental diagnostic tool for a while, and one that is impossible to hurt anyone with or to mess up their diagnosis with."

Broffman, the Pine Street director, hopes to build on the current study to explore the development of an 'electronic nose. "Such technology would attempt to achieve the precision of the dog's nose," he said. "Such technology would also be more likely to appear in your doctor's clinic in time."

Woof

And as if the discoveries were drying up, The Times reported on 3rd January 2014 that Earth's magnetic field may be part of the call of nature that directs the dog's behaviour. After 2,000 observations over two years, scientists found that dogs have a 'highly significant axial preference for north-south alignment during defecation.' Dog's noses act like compass needles. It is highly probably that wolves use magnetic fields to help with navigation and there are lots of anecdotal stories of dogs returning home from large distances. It was after noticing that cows liked to graze in a north-south direction that attention was turned to dogs. Now you may question the value to mankind of research based on dog poo and such mundane observations. However it may be that scientists are seeing the magnetic field as some pattern on the dog's retina. Birds are thought to use it as a map in their migration and maybe dogs are doing the same. If you are a dog owner, you can do your own research with your dog, a compass and of course a collection bag.

Clare Moon, a paediatric diabetes nurse suffers from Type 1 diabetes and hypoglycaemia unawareness, which means she does not feel any symptoms if her sugar levels drop dangerously low. But help is at hand in the form of Magic, 32kg of Labrador jumps up at her and paws her. That's the signal recognising the danger present and Clare responds immediately to her medical needs.

And the Medical Research dog charity has branched out from cancer detection into medical alert dogs. 'Once we realised dogs could do odour detection, we started to think, well, perhaps they can smell other diseases," said Dr Guest. The charity now has 40 dogs alerting their owners to such life-threatening conditions as Addison's disease and severe peanut allergy.

It is looking likely that dogs secrets are still to be fully realised. When they are, if they are ever completely realised, only good can come from them. But to be less head-in-the-clouds what we can say is that the senses of animals are so honed and we really don't understand them at all, but if we can take advantage of them, then we certainly should do so.

Yet what if we put the boot on the other foot? If dogs actually kept humans as pets! Is that worth contemplating? Let me take you on a trip both with surreal and fantasy dimensions.

For £210 you can purchase PetChatz. This dispenses treats and scents and also has a videophone attached. This enables you to see what your dog is doing at any point of the day. Of course if you require seeing how your dog is throughout the day, your employer may question you and your colleagues evaluate your mental health.

I often think of all the horrible and stupid things we do to these miraculous smart animals. And I wonder how we'd like it if our positions were reversed and we became their pets. Perhaps dogs are even planning for this day. After all they do huddle close when they meet. Tiny humans being made to wear tutus and hair bows then sat in a handbag and lady humans continually breeding so that their babies can be sold to any old idiot; humans being chained up all day; humans taught to walk to heel via a sharp kick on the ribs.

Back to reality. Well, does that terrify you or make you appreciate how our relationship should be with dogs? Just who is Taking The Lead?

Chapter 16
Doggerel

The human emotions expressed by sharing a dog's life overflow in many different ways. One which is prevalent is poetry. Let me share some of my **Doggerel**!

Firstly **The SLOW WALK**. I met an elderly woman walking her dog. She was slow. She told me she had been a teacher many years ago but still sees her pupils from time to time. Then I saw her no more.

Secondly **BORDER COLLIES.** This poem came about by seeing a collie pup, bow to his uncle, Tâche. (see pictures)

FOND MEMORIES OF PENNY. My neighbour's Golden Retriever always greeted me when I came back from work, then she met Tâche. They got on well together but sadly Penny died shortly after their initial meeting.

Finally **THE DOG WALK.** A true poem about the remarkable adventures of black Labrador Bobby Dunbar.

THE SLOW WALK

She walked her dog though stooped by old age
Her eyesight was fading removed from each page
No matter the weather each day without fail
In sun and in rain, in snow and in hail
Prince was led on his lead through the park
By the river sometimes but never when dark.

We met now and then through the medium of dogs
Without them I doubt if we'd exchange many words
I learned that she taught many years in the town
And remembered the pupils now they had all grown
Now in her nineties life was beginning to ebb
Both her and on Prince, caught in its web

No walks no lead no dog now to see
The ambulance came to her home around three
The sirens were loud and the lights flashing blue
The mourners formed an orderly queue.
I still walk my dog but I noticed last week
That Prince was enjoying some hide and some seek
A young lad was throwing his ball to and fro
Prince knew at once where to run and to go

Then I thought for a moment on what I was seeing
A change of pace, of trust and of being
What a Best Friend really is.

Border Collies

Old bows to young recalling his puppyhood
Young bows to old respecting authority
Together they communicate silently
Wishing to possess what each other has not
Cousins in nature, living far apart
They meet irregularly but recognise
The breed of the Border collie.
Faithful, obedient and sometimes friendly
Aloof, alert, awaiting instructions
Servant and companion roles perfected
Awaiting my instruction or call to dinner
A satisfaction for man and his dog.

See Tâche with his nephew Tess to appreciate these lines.
Tâche lived in Dumfries while his cousin Tess lived in
Arbroath.

PENNY

At close of day I wandered home
With worries which were many.
My work encompassed grief and strife
But there to greet, was Penny.

She never spoke nor could she
Nor were her signs misleading
We always knew what she would mean
Through loving eyes, just pleading.

But there were times I ran ahead
Passing Penny at some speed
She'd sense Tâche had not eaten all
His bowl was hers - her feed!

Her golden coat and soft brown eyes
Made Penny so appealing
To see her sit and guard "The Grange"
Was a reassuring feeling.

Her pains are over, she's earned her rest
Our sorrows are so many
Yet all our lives are truly blessed
For sharing it with Penny.

THE DOG WALK

Cold nose, warm fur and so happy I must say.
I walk a friend's black Labrador with few words said each
day.
A whistle or a name call, Bobby is his name,
Will distract his attention then he attends to my game.
This time an errant golf ball has strayed out of bounds
Descending to the river, a playground for all hounds.
Bobby sniffs the golfer's scent when he placed the ball on
tee
His swing was rather faulty and with disbelief his eyes did
see.
The ball got ever closer to the fence marked 'Out of
Bounds'
It clipped the golden gorse bush, causing from the tee the
groans.
Across the path then down it fell and landed near the river
The men approached, saw Bobby search and one said,
"Well I never!"
Bobby bounded down the hill and jumped into the water
Bracken snapped and birds flew off, his pace got even
hotter
His jaws retrieved the ball and he sped up with his prey
The grateful blushing golfer smiled, Bobby made his day.
Yet less savoury confrontations have got me off the hook
The tales of Bobby make me wonder if his life could fill a
book.
Bobby's owner is a Police Woman, and that's why he's
called Bobby
And as she's at work and her husband too, walking Bobby
is my hobby.

One day down by the river, it was getting somewhat dark
Three men the worse of drink, were up for every lark
Bobby holds no grudges, but I must confess I felt some
fear.
A timely bark made them halt, and two then dropped their
beer.
"Is he friendly?" they enquired and here I saw my chance.
"He can be," I suggested, but still they did advance.
"He's a Police Officer's dog." Now that cannot be denied.
Yet still I feared their stance. "He sniffs for drugs." I then
conveniently lied.
On hearing this, they turned around unsteady on their feet.
One by one they ran away with guilt to speed retreat.
So Bobby serves a purpose bringing order, love and fun
And if I had four feet, I'd join him on his run.
I'd like his warm fur coat, for all weather conditions too
Not wondering what to wear each day ummm brown or
green or blue?
But a cold nose? No, that would not be so neat
Nor dry dog biscuits or tins of jellied meat.
So let's just honour what we call Man's Best Friend
On each dog, no matter which breed, we really can depend
To cheer us up when we are sad and greet us on returning
A dog makes family life complete and always ever calming.
So Bobby, please remember, that we both enjoy our
walkies
In rain and sleet and sunshine, in sandals, boots and wellies
And when our days on earth are done as all must meet
this fate

I'll still be waiting in my dreams for you at heaven's gate.

Poems © miller caldwell

POST SCRIPT

It is a reality that we live longer than our dogs and so losing a dog is a significant personal and family loss. Others say they could not cope with their short lives and so, dogs are a hassle to them. They can't be taken on holiday or on weekend breaks. Such people see life with their glass half empty. (Some exceptions like the North West Castle Stranraer come to mind and you may find other establishments with an enligntened approach to accepting dogs as guests.)

But these negative reservations become miniscule when a puppy enters your home. Family members often rally round to care for the dog if the owners are on holiday or in hospital and if a summer kennel is the only resort, the standards in kennels are better scrutinised than ever before. Your vet can advise you of good kennels.

Dogs will soon realise it is a temporary placement where many other dogs have found their summer vacation too. The re-unification, as you can imagine, is the most wonderful tactile moment and all is forgiven. It is perhaps best to remain with one kennel, provided you find it good, as familiarity may settle your dog more quickly at its annual temporary abode.

These have been the dogs in my life, so far. Since the passing of Bobby, I have started to walk Blu more regularly. On the first winter walk, Blu swam in the river Nith as anticipated and I thought a large salmon splashed nearby. I was wrong. It was a young inquisitive otter. Blu showed little interest. But the young otter dived and came up closer to inspect Blu. I wished I had my camera that afternoon. Then a kingfisher sped by like a fighter pilot in its steel blue uniform in a shaft of winter light. Without that walk I'd not have seen the magic of nature that day. No two dog walks are ever the same.

Not all have been perfect dogs and much of that can be explained by canine psychology and sometimes by the characteristics of the dog's breed and whether it was a one man dog and not a family pet. Not to have known them however would have been a disadvantage for all dogs deserve their own characteristics and personality just as we have ours.

Mankind has had a relationship with the dog for centuries. That will surely continue. But I hope too we can understand our dogs even better in the years ahead. For in medical advances and in training programmes we are starting to see the value of living with dogs and being treated by dogs. That is something we can look forward to discovering in the years ahead.

Yet perhaps the greatest gift our dogs will give us, is a better understanding of ourselves.

I am his Highness' dog at Kew.
Pray tell me sir, whose dog are you?

On the collar of a dog given by Alexander Pope (1688-1744) to his Royal Highness George II (1727 – 1760).

AUTHOR INTERVIEW

Why did you write a book about dogs?

When the creative mind is alert, it dictates what I write. It is influenced by many different things. For this book I found my father's hand written notes about Glen, his collie. I came across a picture of my mother with her Dalmatian. That got me off to a good start and then I recalled the influence of all the dogs in my life. I realised I had unlocked a store of tales of stories about dogs.

What age group will like this book?

The British public like their animals. Stories such as *Marley,* Bob *the Cat* and *The Way of Muri* have captivated many readers. But these are the stories of individual animals. This book is about many different canine breeds. So rather than identifying an age group, this book will appeal to all dog owners and dog lovers, be they adults or children. Some will be used to the antics of a breed I have known. Others will learn much about other breeds. The book is written in two styles. Part 1 attributes speech to Glen while I attribute thoughts to my dogs in the latter chapters. I leave you to decide which you prefer. But there is nothing to offend in this book and so it can be safely read by all ages, while young children might enjoy seeing the pictures of the dogs in the book and have chapters read to them. They will soon fall asleep dreaming of dogs and of course let sleeping dogs and children lie.

You have written The Parrot's Tale. Do you feature animals or birds in all your books?

Aha! You have got me thinking. Perhaps in every one of my seventeen books there will be a reference to an animal. Animals are, after all, very much part of everyone's lives. My children's books all feature animals prominently viz; Chaz the Friendly Crocodile; Lawrence the Lion Seeks Work; and Danny the Spotless Dalmatian. Children have a fascination with animals.

You have owned a Monkey and a Parrot. Are dogs really your favourite breed of animal?

It is true that I owned a parrot and monkey when I lived in Ghana. These were very special animals too and have much in common in intelligence and understanding with their canine cousins. But for company and companionship, let alone exercise and fresh air, none can beat the dog. Yes, dogs are my favourite animal.

What are you writing now.

One of my short stories, Tell our Sisters, has been shortlisted in an international Short Story competition. As a result it will appear in an anthology of winning stories soon. I am about to write the film script of this story. I have also started an espionage novel. But, of course, I can't tell you anything about that one. Katy Dynes, my illustrator, is working on Danny the Spotless Dalmatian at present and a story about a stolen accordion is at the back of my mind. Now that's not an animal! That makes a change.

Books by the author

NOVELS
> Operation Oboe
> Restless Waves
> The Last Shepherd
> The Parrot's Tale
> Miss Martha Douglas

BIOGRAPHIES
> Poet's Progeny
> Untied Laces – The author's autobiography
> 7 point 7 on the Richter Scale – Diary of the Camp
> Manger at Mundihar in Pakistan NWFP.
> Jim's Retiring Collection
> Take the Lead

SELF HELP
> Have you seen my...Ummm...Memory?
> It's Me, Honest it is. NHS handbook
> Ponderings – short stories and poems in large print.

CHILDREN'S BOOKS
> Chaz the Friendly Crocodile
> Lawrence the Lion Seeks Work
> Danny the Spotless Dalmatian

Miller H. Caldwell

Miller grew up in Kirriemuir in Angus before moving to Glasgow and studied in Edinburgh, Glasgow and London universities.

A former missionary in Tema, Ghana, Miller has been a humanitarian worker all his life. He was the Regional and then first Authority Reporter to the Children's Hearings for Dumfries & Galloway before becoming the writer in residence at Dumfries Prison. In 2002 in London he received the Crannog Community Care award. In 2006 in Islamabad he recieved the Muslim Hands International Award for humanitarian work after being the camp manager at Mundihar. He has been a full time author since 2003. One of his recent short stories has been short listed in an International Short Story competition. He is married with two daughters and lives in Dumfries. He regularly gives talks about being an author and about his life.

List of Supporters

Artemis Scotland   Cultural and Educational Services
Authorsonline.co.uk   Publishing Life's Next Chapter
Bard Vets Ltd   Dumfries Veterinary Services
Barnhill Joinery   No Job Too Small
Brewin Dolphin   Discretionary Wealth Managers
Dumfries and Galloway Canine Rescue Centre
The Scottish Fire & Rescue Service Dumfries.
The Sign Centre   Dumfries
Tony Clark   Plumbing and Heating Engineer
Trevor Knowles   HK Financial Advisers
Your Move   UK Estate Agency Dumfries

Lightning Source UK Ltd.
Milton Keynes UK
UKOW06f0536150914

238487UK00010BA/75/P